DEEP TRAVEL

SOUVENIRS FROM THE INNER JOURNEY

Edited by
Anna Elkins & Christina Ammon

Deep Travel LLC
150 Rocky Knoll Lane
Jacksonville, OR 97530
info@deeptravelworkshops.com

Cover photo by Tim Daw of Christina Ammon's great-grandmother's travel map

Cover & book design by Anna Elkins

First edition: July 2019

ISBN: 9781099257124

Printed in the United States of America

The true journey is within.

Contents

Acknowledgments

With enormous gratitude to the mentors, teachers, and colleagues at the Book Passage Travel Writers & Photographers Conference. From you we learned to travel deeply.

Introduction by Anna Elkins

While traveling on the single nib of a shoestring in my twenties, I heard the travel maxim: take only photos, leave only footprints. I mostly took this to heart. I have very few tangible things from that season: a small, wooden star ornament from a Christmas market in the Swiss Alps; a vintage postcard of Notre-Dame from a *bouquiniste* in Paris; and a maroon GDR-era tracksuit jacket from a thrift shop in East Berlin. But what I value most are the journals I brought home, packed with words.

Not long after those travels, I returned to Europe to spend several seasons as a ghostwriter in a Catalonian village on the Mediterranean. It sounds glamorous, but it was simple, and I was willing to work for room and board. My employer was an American expat married to a French-Swiss woman, and the couple had spent summers in their little Spanish coastal home since their children were young. The house situated way up above the rocky *calas*, steep on a seaside mountain, accessed by stone staircases and paths that linked the neighborhood to the town below.

We became great friends, and after morning work, we would descend the dirt paths between wild, waist-high tumbles of lavender and anise to the beach cove for a swim. One day, the woman and I walked down together, talking. In her French accent, she told me how her children had loved their summers in that family house. She said, "They made us promise to never sell it. My daughter told me it was the best souvenir."

I had heard her use the word *souvenir* before in ways that surprised me. In that moment, I realized that, in French, souvenir means memory.

That moment of knowing is forever with me: the back of my friend's head as she walked ahead of me, the lavender hitting my calves, sending its fragrance into the afternoon air. A new layer of a word I thought I knew coming closer like the nearing sea.

Since then, every time I hear *souvenir*, I think of what we choose to remember—what we choose to bring back from our travels, our lives.

◆ ◆ ◆

When Christina Ammon, founder of Deep Travel, suggested that we compile an anthology of writings from five years of workshops, I was interested—but also a bit apprehensive. I knew how much work it would take to get from idea to hardcopy. Yet I also knew this would be a beautiful way to celebrate the words we gather on our travels.

And as the submissions came in, I fell in love. I fell in love with sacred geometry in the Fez Medina. I fell in love with *las palmas* and their coconuts in Yelapa. I fell in love with *flamenco puro* in the *gitano* caves above Granada.

This book brims with work by over forty contributors, including Deep Travel instructors Erin Byrne, Larry Habegger, Dot Fisher-Smith, and Lavinia Spalding—and also Christina and myself, who often teach on the trips.

Each piece of writing and every photo inside this book is a souvenir. It may be a souvenir of mishap or redemption, of misunderstanding or revelation, of despair or delight—or a mix of all.

Words last longer than things ever could. Words are

lighter to pack than a Moroccan rug, better for the environment than an Eiffel Tower key chain, and easier to share widely than a bottle of mezcal—all good reasons to travel deeply with writing.

May what we bring back from our travels be a gift for ourselves and for others. The souvenirs in these pages are such gifts. It is a joy to help bring them home.

Introduction by Christina Ammon

A few years ago, my boyfriend and I bought a van in England with the idea to convert it into a camper. Our plan was to ferry it to Morocco, drive overland through Mauritania, and on into Mali. A camper van seemed to me the perfect way to travel: by literally sitting at the wheel of our own adventure, we could stop where we wanted to stop and stay where we wanted to stay. We could see the world on our own terms. At least, that was the idea.

We stationed ourselves to do the van conversion in Tarifa, a gusty town on the southern tip of Spain where we'd scored a house-sitting gig. The apartment reeked of cigarette smoke and was outfitted with a saggy, inflatable couch, but we were grateful: with a complete kitchen and hot shower, it would be a comfortable-enough home base to work from. And so we settled in, established a routine, and dove immediately into our project. Each morning, I'd feed electric chords from the third floor balcony down to the parking lot where my boyfriend stood amid his wrenches, plywood, and power tools. While he got to work crafting a bed and countertops for the van, I agreeably took care of the domestic duties.

I shopped for groceries at the Lidl market down the block. There I gathered coffee, fresh produce, and marveled daily at a vending machine that dispensed fresh baguettes. While cruising the aisles for dinner ideas, I often met other overland travelers stocking up on last-minute wine and cheese before undertaking their own crossings to Morocco. I noted their travel tips, listened to their stories, and when I finished my shopping, went outside to admire their van set-ups. From that high parking lot aerie at the Lidl market, grocery bags in hand, I could see all the way across the Strait of Gibraltar to the Rif Mountains in Morocco. My adrenals surged with excitement. The freedom of the road lay ahead, and very soon I'd be hashtagging #VanLife all over my sun-drenched Facebook posts.

Well, not very soon. The van conversion took much longer than expected; there were design challenges and mechanical problems requiring mail-order parts. I managed my impatience and flagging sense of purpose by cooking unnecessarily elaborate meals and leafing through the self-help books that lined the apartment's shelves. I also forced myself outside for long, wind-beaten walks each afternoon. While I'd imagined southern Spain to be sunny place to overwinter—a place to lay on the beach—mostly I found myself hunkered behind Tarifa's old walls and battlements, feeling not the levity of being on vacation, but the same deep Andalusian melancholy that haunted the work of Lorca and no doubt inspired the dark arts of bullfighting. Days crawled by, the van wasn't done, and eventually my EU visa expired. "You'll need to go to Morocco now," my boyfriend said. His British passport didn't have the same restrictions. "I'll meet you in Tangier with the camper in a few days."

The next morning, I boarded the ferry alone and nested up in a cheap Tangier hotel for four days. Then five. Then eight. I wandered the Grand Socco, snooped through the iconic El Minzah hotel, visited a mosque, and plodded around the beach on a camel while a tout took my picture. *The part still hasn't arrived*, my boyfriend would message. Restless now, I took one last, long look across the strait at

Spain and then turned my heart and mind south, boarding a bus to the mountain town of Chefchaouen. There I formed a despondent and lonely figure, filling my time by wandering its blue byways and idling alone in the cafés. Then I pushed onward to the city of Fez. When I entered the 9,000 passageways of its ancient medina, I found myself not just physically lost, but also psychically lost. My despair peaked. My boyfriend still had no ETA. I craved companionship like food and water.

I passed the long hours in my hostel reading *A House in Fez* by Suzanna Clarke, a book that insightfully depicts the process of restoring an old *riad* in the medina. In a bid to connect, I sent her an email. She replied. We met for dinner, and upon hearing my predicament, she and her husband Sandy invited me to stay at their house.

The next morning, they led me up the stairs to my room. Looking at the hand-painted ceiling and ornate, wrought-iron windows, I had the magical sense of being ushered right into the pages of her book. From the bed, I could hear morning birdsong and nearly reach out and pluck an orange from the courtyard tree I'd read so much about. Over the next couple of weeks, we formed a tight little family, drinking coffee and writing together in the mornings and indulging in wine and movies and petting the cats in the evenings. Sometimes, Sandy and I put on *The Grateful Dead,* and I'll never forget him twirling around the living room in his wool *djellaba.*

By the time my boyfriend pulled the camper van up to the walls of the medina, I'd established my own life in Fez. I could expertly navigate the twists and turns of our corner of the old city and scrimmage through the souk to get my shopping done. I even had a set of friends: Omar, the photographer; Sam, a Fulbright scholar studying *djinns;* Mike, a British expat who ran a local cross-cultural café.

Sandy and Suzanna eventually left for a trip to Brazil and

my boyfriend and I stayed on to take care of their house and feed their cats. We never embarked on our overland drive through Mauritania or Mali—and in fact eventually broke up. But in retrospect, all of our failed overland plans yielded fruit; in those weeks wandering alone and then staying in one place, I got to know Morocco more deeply than I'd ever imagined. The groundwork for our first Deep Travel workshop was laid.

◆◆◆

Now, several years later, I'm in the middle of planning Deep Travel's eighth workshop to Morocco. As I ponder routes and accommodation picks for the group, I notice my strong impulse to squeeze all the discomfort and unpredictability from the journey. I try to compose every hour of the trip like writing sheet music for a symphony; I want the red spring poppies to be blooming on the day we drive through the countryside, I want the luggage donkeys to arrive exactly as the van pulls up to the town gate so there is no awkward waiting around, and I scheme for the Sufi band to strike up the minute we arrive to the celebration dinner. I check the weather constantly, willing it to be just right when we are having our picnic among the ruins at Volubilis, and I even consult the cosmos, googling up the season's sunset hours to ensure that the just-right wine is served on the just-right terrace right as the perfect sunset pinkens the sky over the hills of Moulay Idriss. Then I carefully calibrate the schedule in an attempt to maneuver the group's mood as well, balancing alone time with together time, alternating the exotic and edgy with the familiar and comfortable.

I am vexed by this controlling impulse. After all, the biggest rewards of my own travel came from things *not* going according to plan—from things going flat-out wrong. If the van conversion had gone smoothly, we'd have driven self-sufficiently cross-country and I'd have never met Sandy and Suzanna or have come to know the Fez Medina. And it's not just me. Over several years of hosting workshops, I've noticed that some of the richest experiences and writings come when the participants have to parse out their own disappointments; their room isn't what they wanted, they lost a beloved camera, or a travel companion is wearing on them. It is in this vulnerable place—let down, exposed and often in need of help—that we are primed to receive the gifts of travel: the unexpected friend, the sharpening of our senses in a moment of fear, the uncommon grace of an innkeeper helping us through a day of illness.

This theme runs through many of the stories in this anthology. In "The Whole Desert is a Living Souk," Fernando Manrique realizes that the silent Sahara of his fantasies is not so silent after all. In "Jackpot," adventurer Ruby Hanes decides on happiness while navigating the ups and downs of Yelapa. Just when Stacy Boyington doubts she's a writer, she finds the perfect metaphor in her story "Taza Azul." And if you think getting in a taxi with strangers in Morocco is a bad idea, Tania Amochaev might change your mind in her story "Do You Remember Me?" In almost all of the stories in this book, the writers arrive with an expectation or belief only to have it dismantled by travel sprites that seem to find good humor in messing with our plans.

◆ ◆ ◆

Last spring, my co-worker Anna and I sat in the lobby of our Tangier hotel and looked across the Strait of Gibraltar toward Spain. The wind ripped through the trees outside, keeping us from the loungers out on the veranda. We were with a Deep Travel group and, aside from the turbulent weather, we'd all hit a tough spot: there were uncooperative showers, sore knees, fatigue, and the fish restaurant we'd whetted their appetites for all year was closed. I battled an encroaching sense of defeat, intensely aware that the writers flew a long way and spent a lot of money to come on this workshop.

In these moments of second-guessing, I often wonder if, rather than trying to hand-stitch our itineraries in the idealistic spirit of artisans bent on providing something one-of-a-kind, we would be better off working with big travel companies and their smoothed-out package tours. But who wants to be herded onto a giant, air-conditioned bus to a characterless hotel at the edge of town for a bland meal? Even then, there are no guarantees: a tire could blow out at any moment.

The truth is, discomfort in travel is unavoidable. In fact, trouble is built into the very word *travel* if you trace its etymology back to its 14th-century root word, *travail,* meaning difficulty, or labor. Trouble—or "the ordeal"—also shows up as a key passage of The Hero's Journey that Joseph Campbell described so well in his research into mythology.

Feeling slightly defeated in that Tangier lobby, I looked across the strait and remembered the failed camper van trip from so long ago. The idea that I can steer my own adventure—or anyone else's for that matter—suddenly strikes me as absurd. John Steinbeck had it right when he said, "People don't take trips—trips take people." This is probably a good thing. It's why travel remains interesting, even when all corners of the planet are crowded with tourists. Despite all the other pilgrims on the Camino de Santiago, the crowds packing the Sistine Chapel, and the processions climbing the Eiffel Tower, travel still does its work on our soul—dashing our expectations and then sneaking up on us from behind with the perfect gift.

In the end, travel corners us and ask us to expand. It asks us to get resourceful because sometimes you set out to have an epic overland drive across Africa, but the van won't start, the part doesn't arrive, and you end up on a ferry alone heading toward the shores of Tangier. Then you might find yourself living in a house in Fez, a cat purring in your lap, considering what it means to stay put and really get to know a place—considering what it means to not just travel far but, ultimately, to travel deep.

*Christina Ammon & Anna Elkins at Shakespeare & Company—
beginning research for a future Deep Travel Paris workshop*

The Himalayas, Nepal
Photo by Christina Ammon

PART ONE

Nepal

Deep Travel Nepal

In December of 2014, Deep Travel took a journey into the art of writing and philanthropy. We landed in Kathmandu and stayed at the most sacred Buddhist site in Southeast Asia, the Boudhanath Stupa. We shared chai in the tent village of an evolving migrant community. We drove to Pokhara for a short trek in the Annapurna region and visited mountain villages. We dialogued with conservationists working to protect the endangered Himalayan Vulture—and even paraglided with them wing-to-wing! We walked along the scenic Phewa Lake, savored traditional *dal bhat,* and wrote while looking up at the Himalayas. By trip's end, Deep Travel had truly engaged "The Roof of the World."

MJ Pramik parahawking in Nepal

When There's No Time Left for Fear

MJ PRAMIK

When I hit sixty, my eldest daughter said, "Sixty is the new forty." These words spawned in me a wanderlust the likes of which I couldn't believe. Weeks after my birthday, I challenged myself to travel alone to Antarctica. After cavorting with flocks of frenzied penguins and climbing out of a dormant volcano, I arrived to Ushuaia in Tierra del Fuego—and an email bearing the news that my ninety-one-year-old father was fading fast. I rushed from Argentina to Ohio to hold his hand for the last five days of his life. I never did tell him, a great watcher of birds, about my adventure with the penguins that he would have so loved.

After witnessing his death, I resolved to live more fully in each moment. My happiest twinklings now come when I'm somewhere new, moving through uncharted waters. Not only did I commit to hitting the road more frequently each year, I pledged to my father's memory to let go of fears that, at sixty, still held me back.

I have a particular fear of heights. Even Ferris wheels stop me cold. My breath freezes whenever the bucket pauses at the top. I have peered warily at the London Eye, never gathering the gumption to purchase a ticket; similarly, I have always adamantly refused to look down from the Empire State Building, and even when flying I automatically select an aisle seat.

But having watched my father face death with grace and courage, I now vowed to face life without the reticence and trepidation that had tugged at me for a lifetime. It was in this spirit of abandon that I pulled a running jump off the 5,291-foot high Sarangkot Mountain in Nepal, parahawking with a bird named Kevin.

◆ ◆ ◆

Before I went to Nepal, the concept of parahawking was entirely foreign to me. The British falconer Scott Mason and his crew created this hybrid of falconry and paragliding in 2001, melding adventure with conservation. The Parahawking Project educates visitors about hawk and vulture flight behaviour and how these birds survive in the wild. Through tandem parahawking rides, the organization raises funds to restore the nearly decimated vulture population in Nepal.

Vultures have an enduring image problem. People often envision them circling above a nearly dead animal, ready to dive in once it heaves its last breath. On top of humans' general distaste for these creatures, a crisis occurred in the late 1990s when Nepalese, Indian, and Pakistani farmers treated their farm animals with the anti-inflammatory diclofenac to reduce their arthritic pain as they aged. When the medicated animals eventually died in the open, the vultures that feasted on carrion were then poisoned by the diclofenac. As a result, their numbers decreased precipitously.

Parahawking consists of paragliding while feeding water buffalo meat to a large raptor. You hang suspended in a seat while a seasoned paraglider pilot sits behind you and operates the guide lines and controls. One of the raptors flown in Scott's Parahawking Project is Kevin, a trained, white-feathered Egyptian vulture whose black-tipped wings were a stunning sight to behold, spanning five-and-a-half feet.

Kevin is a rescue bird. The Egyptian vulture, which inhabits southern Europe, northern Africa, and western and southern Asia, is one of ten species nearing extinction. On Phewa Lake, Scott's home base, Kevin demonstrated his species' expertise at the use of tools by dropping rocks onto an egg to crack the shell. His thin beak and long neck allow him to claim carrion larger birds cannot.

Kevin and his winged friends were born to fly, but I wasn't. Choosing to soar off a cliff was not my usual modus operandi. I required a slight coaxing. Christina, organizer of my Nepal expedition, encouraged me. "They haven't lost anyone yet," she said. *But there's always the first time*, the fearful doubter in me replied, albeit under my breath.

However, my sixty-year-new resolve allowed another rather surprising thought: if I must die someday, soaring through the wind currents above the white Annapurnas will be as lovely a place as any.

And in the days leading up to the event, I continued trekking the sites around Pokhara, panting my way up to the Shanti Stupa, or Peace Pagoda, the Buddhist shrine on an island in the lake adjoining Pokhara. The stunning view of the Annapurnas kept me in the present.

My only instructions for parahawking were: leap off the cliff and keep running in case the chute doesn't open. *Right.* My mind tried to force my legs to move though the huge and powerful wind gusts. I was slammed back into my harness seat, and a crew member had to help our tandem launch… and then we were off, circling the Sarangkot area with two dozen other paragliders.

In flight, we soared eye-to-eye with the enormous birds,

following their movements to catch updrafts and keep our chute apparatus aloft. The eyesight of birds betters that of humans by ten to fifteen times. Their keen eyes identified the swirls of dust-defining drafts and currents that were invisible to me on this bright, blue-skied day.

Suspended in the air, time stopped. Scott swooped up, whistled for Kevin. The graceful vulture made his approach to my outstretched, leather-gloved hand that held his treat. He gently retrieved the fresh-cut water buffalo chunk that would fuel his long journeys through the air. We repeated this scene many times. I breathed deeply each of the thirty minutes aloft.

One abrupt updraft did surprise me. I had to close my eyes and trust my pilot during a quick right jolt and ascent. We climbed several hundred feet fast, then turned, and the entire snow-capped Annapurna range spread out before us.

The sky resplendent with multi-coloured chutes, I found I had no time to even consider my fear.

Our half-hour flight ended so gently. Much like Kevin, we glided to a small patch of grass bordering Phewa Lake, smack-dab across the road from the impressive Maya Devi Temple. Enlightenment indeed.

I find myself agreeing more and more with my sometime traveling companion, an Australian septuagenarian whose motto is: "Comfort travel doesn't interest me." If anything, I now seek *discomfort travel*, or travel that offers me opportunities to confront my fears, push my boundaries, expand my worldview and build trust and connections with my fellow creatures on this earth.

I hear some people speak of bucket lists and thousands of places to see before they leave this earth, as if travel exists as a checklist to complete. I find that each second spent traveling breathes life into the following moment of time and place. I now see the distinct shape of each leaf on the trees lining my street and inhale the scent of cantaloupe in my local market with gratitude. I meditate while watching the birds gliding above my San Francisco home. Traveling deepens one's senses and sense of self. It lengthens and stretches out the time we have to challenge ourselves to begin anew, each day to rise above this earth.

Prayer flags across a Himalayan valley
Photo by Christina Ammon

I Close my Eyes to See the World

ANNA ELKINS

We leave Kathmandu by bus
on a smog-sunny afternoon
after watching cremations
across Bagmati River.

I lay a thin scarf along
my west-facing arm.
Beneath the dark cotton,
my skin looks the color of ash.

But I am alive.
I close my eyes.
In the lull & lurch of rough road,
I doze.

The city goes on for traffic hours.
I open my eyes
to steep villages,
to rice terraces lipping down the hills.

I close my eyes.
The scarf above my body

becomes a prayer flag
kissing my skin.

The bus steels to a stop.
I open my eyes in a sleepy blink
& think I see a strand of the flags
smiling across a rooftop.

But no—a line of laundry
bright with the same five colors—
clothing for bodies belonging
to spirits I'll never meet.

I close my eyes on this bus
full of people wrapped in prayers,
wondering at our highest arrival.
Behind our eyes, worlds begin.

Boatman on Lake Phewa
Photo by Christina Ammon

The Himalayas
Photo by Molly McKissick

Himalayan Potatoes

LARRY HABEGGER

The Sherpa woman glared down from above the unmarked trail junction where I stood uncertain which way to go. Her black eyes stared through me as if I were a ghost.

"*Keni hinang* Nang? *Lam ga* Nang?" I asked in phrasebook Sherpa and Tibetan, gesturing toward one trail and then the other. Then I tried Nepali: "*Kun bato* Nang?" Finally, English: "Which way to Nang?"

Her look seemed full of some deeply rooted hostility that had found a place to rest. I had no idea if I was communicating anything, but a shiver ran through me. She wasn't going to tell me which trail went to Nang. She was silent as rock, immobile.

Traveling without a guide, my friend Neil and I were off the most popular trekking route heading up a side valley to Mount Everest. We hadn't been concerned until now because the routes were clear, and we knew we could get food along the way at the lodges or from locals happy to earn some money. But we were down to our last few scraps, and we had a long way to go.

We shrugged, agreed on the lower trail, and went on our way. Despite the heavy pack on my back, I couldn't shake the chill that had settled upon me, and the longer we walked the more I wondered if the chill was as much from the strange encounter with the Sherpani as the clinging fog that had crept up the canyon. I began to mull stories Nepali friends had told me of evil spirits that preyed on vulnerable beings, and I wondered if I was vulnerable, if I'd done something to bring this ill omen into our path. I walked on, following Neil, cold, hungry, uneasy.

The trail gradually descended. Fog drifted down the canyon walls, shrouding us. The sound of the river below had grown from a faint backdrop to a constant growling companion. An hour later we stopped and ate our final crackers.

"What did you make of that woman back there?" I asked.

"Strange. Made me wonder if she even knew we were there."

A puff of damp breeze penetrated my three layers of clothing. "I felt like she saw us all right, but wanted nothing to do with us."

"Yeah, she probably has a hundred trekkers a day asking directions."

"I suppose," I said, but it felt deeper than that.

A moment later I struggled to rise, hardly noticing that Neil was already making his way down the trail. One foot in front of the other, I reminded myself, my mantra for trekking in Nepal. The fog clung to the trees, an icy tongue deepening my chill.

Soon we could see the river at the bottom of the chasm, a churning, gray torrent stripping the land and sweeping glacier dust from the flanks of Everest. Still we had seen no one else, nor any sign of human habitation. Then the trail broke off at the site of an enormous gash in the canyon, a landslide that had taken half a mountain with it. Neil was staring grimly at the near-vertical slope we had to cross when I caught up with him. My legs felt like lead, and by the look of things we had no choice but to turn back. My heart sank. We'd find no food or shelter by going back. We'd walked too far and couldn't possibly climb out of the canyon before dark. But how could we proceed?

Neil thought he saw a way. "Look, the hillside's soft, we can plant our feet. Take it slow and we'll make it."

With a heavy pack to balance I didn't see how, but I was too tired to argue. One slip would mean a fast slide down a hundred feet to the boulders and that roiling current. But we had little choice, and Neil set out.

He dug in his boot, then planted the next one in a timid step, then another, and another until he was moving slowly across the slide, leaving bootprints for me to follow.

Unsteadily I took a step, then another. Pebbles dislodged and sluiced down the hillside to the rocks below, their sounds absorbed by the roar of the river. The weight of the pack bore down, and I tried to keep it from shifting, certain that one misstep would send me tumbling along the same path as those pebbles. I glanced up to see Neil halfway across, fifty feet from me, and that gave me hope. I concentrated, wobbled once when my pack shifted, but caught myself with a flash of adrenaline. Sweat dripped down my face. The pack straps dug into my shoulders. The thin air made my head swim. But I kept moving, and an eternity later looked up to see Neil standing on firm ground at the end of the slide, only twenty feet away.

A few more steps and I was across. The instant I touched solid ground, I shed my pack and collapsed, needing many minutes to regain my composure. Sweat soaked my whole body, stealing what little warmth I had. Down in this cold canyon, daylight was fading and we had to keep going to find shelter.

Neil urged me up and we set off again. I was woozy now, not sure why we were plodding along this way, even where we were and why. I'd spent enough time in the wilderness to know that the bony grip of hypothermia was latching on to me, and I tried to calm myself. Need food. Warmth. Rest.

Then Neil shouted. He'd spotted a hut ahead. Two, three, perhaps a village, but certainly food and shelter. He rushed on, and I kept up my mantra, step-by-step. When I arrived at the first stone hut, Neil's sullen look told me everything I needed to know. The place was deserted. Again I collapsed, this time against a cold stone wall, too tired to contemplate moving.

But then Neil shouted again. The third hut was open, we could get out of the fog. I dragged myself up and stumbled the few feet to the hut where I dropped everything in a heap. Dim light edged in through tiny windows, but the place was dry, full of straw, and not nearly as cold as outside. We finished off our water, climbed into our sleeping bags, and lay down for the long wait till morning.

Sleeping at high altitude is never easy, and I spent hours shivering until my body generated enough heat to allow the down bag to warm me up. At some point I was aware that I wasn't freezing anymore, and then I slept, waking to faint light that suggested a new day.

My stomach ached, but not from the intestinal problems that afflict most trekkers in Nepal. I needed food.

Our maps revealed that we should have been much higher than we were, and we realized we must have taken the wrong trail and ended up in a summer herders' camp, abandoned now for the approaching winter. Would that mean that the villages ahead would be deserted as well? We needed to climb out of the canyon and keep going with the faith that we'd find the main trail, and someone still there who would sell us food.

With no other option, we began bushwhacking up the hillside. Eventually we found a trail that seemed to be leading us up, and as we trudged along, the track became clearer. Better yet, high above, the first rays of sunshine graced the hillside. Blue sky emerged where we'd seen only fog the day before.

We climbed out of the forest and steadily up. I kept looking ahead, hoping to see where the path would flatten out on the main trail. Then I thought I saw someone sitting on the rocks high above. With every step I looked again, trying to convince myself that yes, it was a person, but fearing the shattering disappointment if it turned out to be just a trick of the light, a gargoyle staring out into the canyon. We climbed, mule-like, and with every step what I saw continued to look like a person.

And then it moved. Yes! It was a man, resting on a stone wall in the glorious sunshine, watching our slow progress with surprise, amusement, anger, indifference? Who cared?

When we reached him, the old man slid off the wall as nimbly as a cat. Before we could speak, he motioned for us to follow him, gesturing at his mouth and then to us to ask if we were hungry. We didn't need to answer. We followed him through the sunshine to his stone hut ablaze with morning light.

He offered us seats on a bench covered with a Tibetan carpet. A fire burned in his earthen stove, sending wafts of smoke curling to the ceiling and out the thatched roof. Sunlight streamed through the window and threw halos around him. Deep lines carved his face into a mask of toil, but tranquility shone in his eyes.

In a tin basin, he washed his hands over and over, taking several minutes as if in a ritual cleansing, then poured water into a black pot and put it on the stove. Then he took a bag of potatoes off the wall and gently removed them and put them on a tin plate. With a small brush, he carefully scrubbed every speck of dirt off each potato, one by one, until they gleamed. The pile of potatoes glowing in the sunlight, and the care with which he handled this food, made me feel we were in a sanctified presence.

From that moment I watched every move he made, my hunger forgotten, marveling at the precision with which he cleaned the cups into which he would pour our tea, the delicacy of his actions when slicing the potatoes, the patient care he took to polish every spoon and fork and plate before he placed them, just so, before us. Here was a man who treated hospitality—the preparation of a simple meal for guests—as a higher calling.

We sat for an hour or more in that warm hut watching this patient yak herder prepare a simple dish of fried potatoes. When I took the first sip of tea, when I inhaled the first scent of those potatoes, when I tasted the first nibble of that life-saving meal, I discovered the true meaning of gratitude.

The sun beamed straight into the canyon when we finally rose to leave. Belly full, energy restored, I hoisted my pack to continue along the trail. And then I remembered the woman who had caused me so much anxiety the day before. She was our messenger as well as our nemesis, setting up our encounter with this man who taught me a lesson in kindness and the importance of every detail. He was the yang to her yin, the two of them the whole we all seek, the crazy mad jumble that is our humanity.

We all have our own doses of light and dark, and that thought, along with the memory of those simple but exquisite potatoes, left me feeling lighter than I had in days as we headed up the trail toward Everest.

A different version of this story appeared in *A Moveable Feast: Life-Changing Food Adventures Around the World* (Lonely Plant, 2010).

Receiving a blessing at the end of a trek
Photo by Maria Bitarello

Photo by Tree Knowlton

Tree Knowlton has joined us for many workshops. Her niece made this charm for her before she joined Deep Travel Nepal in 2014, and she has brought it on all of her Deep Travel adventures since.

Do Not Bury the Dead

MARIA BITARELLO

We must admit there will be music despite everything.
—from "A Brief for the Defense" by Jack Gilbert

The first tragic loss in my life was Saul. We were both 12, and he was accidently shot by another child, a neighbor who found his mother's gun and fired from a window. Saul's family is very close to mine, and his death has, ever since, become a part of our lives. Of who I am. I cannot separate myself from that girl who was told before school, one September morning, that her friend was killed. We are the same.

The second tragic loss I experienced was that of my cousin, Daniela. I was a sophomore in college and she was 15 when her younger brother found her in her bedroom, breathless from an accidental chloroform overdose. Some say her death was avoidable, but it makes no difference whose fault it was. She's not here. And that is the all-encompassing truth.

The third tragic loss was Jorge, a good friend from college who died a couple of years after we graduated. He was in the advanced stages of AIDS and did not know he was sick until two weeks prior to his death. He was harshly judged by many, but the truth is that he was a beautiful man. And beauty deserves no punishment.

The fourth one was tough. Roberta and I were both 27 when she committed suicide and took with her memories that only the two of us shared. She was my oldest friend. With her went a part of me that no one else knows, and I felt amputated. Abandoned. For a while, I hated her for having brought that amount of pain and incomprehension into my life. I will never fully understand her decision, but I know it prevented me from ignoring death, and also suicide. Her swift and violent departure became a layer of my skin. And not only can I not imagine myself without this experience, I don't want to. It taught me that I don't need to understand in order to accept it. This loss, apart from all others, has been the single most brutal, real, and liberating. It awakened me to mortality and, consequently, to life. And for this, I feel gratitude.

The fifth tragic loss in my life was Bruno, a high school friend. He succumbed to the injuries brought on by having nearly his entire body carbonized after a car crash. He was generous and kind, and he reminded me that we cannot take with us anything from this life, this world. Not even our bodies, our vehicles of pleasure and pain, without which there is no life.

Lastly were two tragic losses that loved ones close to me experienced. Eugénie was younger than me and died from a brain tumor at 25. She craved life. And Alexandre was in his mid thirties and died in a plane crash. He was a gentle, loving soul. From them I learned that there will always be something left unsaid, undone, incomplete. And closure will come despite of it.

◆ ◆ ◆

We go through life creating bonds. With people. Places. Stories. And then we have to let them go, one by one. Unlike what we are told as children, death does not greet us only at the end. It doesn't happen in the distant future, when we die. Death is all around us, all the time. And our own is but the last. Everyone I know will die. Everyone who has lived has died. Everyone still alive will also die. And so will I.

Knowing this fills me with release, surrender. Or faith is perhaps a better word. Not knowing when or how it will occur still allows me to accept and trust its inescapable and necessary quality. And this, alone, makes every living moment unique and a once-only experience. Good or bad, everything is a part of the living realm and, therefore, precious and worthwhile. Feeling sad and grieving takes its toll after some time, and we tire ourselves out of sadness. The same comes from bliss or contentment. It too will pass. And that's OK.

In Portuguese, we have a word, *saudades*, which is difficult to translate into other languages. In English, we say we miss someone; in French, someone is missing from us. *Saudades*, however, conveys more than longing or nostalgia. It can be and often is a pleasant sensation. Because if you experience *saudades* from a loved one, it is the very affirmation that there is something to be missed: that the love in which you two are embalmed is the same feeling that you wish kept you company at this moment.

I like this word, and there is something to be learned from the Portuguese poets in times of grief. When we loose someone, his or her absence is overpowering. And yet, in the lusophone world, we are taught to not discard our dead. *Saudades* makes their absence present. Pain can be transformed; grief will no longer be frightening; the dead may live on in our hearts and groins. And we need never be alone.

Boudhanath Stupa in Kathmandu, Nepal
Photo by Maria Bitarello

Far, Far Away

MOLLY MCKISSICK

In Nepal prayer wheels are turning,
churning like clicking teeth.

By the lights of butter lamps burning
for the prayers of wandering pilgrims.

For the mothers and fathers and children
clockwise 'round the great Boudha Stupa.

Circumambulating the "Wish-Granting Jewel"
again, and again, and again.

Circling, the well-worn path knows
the footsteps of pray-ers praying

by the millions for thousands of years,
treading prayers with their hearts full of yearning.

In Nepal the prayer wheels are turning
like the clicking of teeth, they are churning.

By the lights of butter lamps burning.
The whole world is a prayer wheel turning.

Photo by Molly McKissick

Admiring quilts in the tent village of Kathmandu
Photo by Christina Ammon

Happily Ever After?

CHRISTINA AMMON

I've always wondered if it was just a cliché: are people in developing countries really happier than we are? How many times have friends returned from their travels saying, "They were poor but they seemed so much happier"?

Or is this just something we say to feel better about the inequities of the world? To offset the discomfort of drinking cappuccinos that cost the equivalent of a full day's labor in Nepal?

Which, I must confess, is exactly what I was doing the other morning near the Boudanath Stupa in Kathmandu. When dining in Nepal, the whole when-in-Rome axiom doesn't apply. For me, at least, *tarkari* soup at the local breakfast joint delivers a bacterial karate-chop that drops me to the bathroom floor for three days.

So I sipped my fancy coffee and chewed a croissant and surveyed the scene from an outdoor café seat. My friend, James Hopkins, would arrive at 8:00. We planned to visit a nearby tent village where he's befriended a group of beggars by helping them start a quilt-making business.

◆ ◆ ◆

It was a busy morning at Boudha. Seekers make the

pilgrimage to this holiest Buddhist site in Southeast Asia from faraway places to walk clockwise *koras*—or circles—around the dome of the stupa. They spin prayer wheels and sprinkle marigolds and blood-red *tikka* powder on the surrounding statues to gain karmic merit.

This morning there were two very different *koras* underway.

Closest to the stupa, an inner *kora* of red-robed monks shuffled along with strands of prayer beads swaying from their fingertips. For some it seemed a perfunctory morning stroll, while others worked their way around the stupa in arduous prostrations, dropping to their knees and touching their foreheads to the ground in a sort of traveling sun salutation.

While these devotees mumbled prayers and made offerings, on the outer rung of Boudanath, a *kora* of tourists and touts stirred into action. Shopkeepers unlocked their doors and heaped wares along the street: postcards, incense, tiger balm, and plastic prayer beads. At gear shops, trekkers began fitting boots and sunglasses. They fingered the fleece of knock-off North Face jackets and occasionally turned to snap pictures of the stupa in the changing morning light.

Are they happiers or not? The members of the inner *kora* with their simple offerings of mantras and marigolds, or the affluent outer *kora*, coddled by down jackets and cappuccinos?

"Happier? I think they are more content," James observed. He'd just arrived. Tall, light-skinned, and blonde, James was clearly an outsider. Still, he is as familiar as one might hope to get with a culture so different from our own. He's long been studying Buddhism in Kathmandu and is an assistant to the revered teacher, Chökyy Nima Rinpoche. And his quilt project has put James squarely in the middle of social dynamics of some of the poorest city dwellers.

"Yeah, they fight—but there is a level of contentment that

we don't have. They are in the company their whole extended family."

We sipped our coffees and watched as momentum gathered around the stupa. It was morning rush hour at Boudanath, and the inner *kora* was turning into a red whir of monks putting miles on their legs and on the prayer wheels.

"What they also have is devotion," James said. In his observation, Westerners approach Buddhism more cerebrally and are deft at analyzing the intricate concepts, such as "no-self"—the idea that people have no fixed-self, but are instead an ever-changing collection of moods and preferences. The local Tibetans have more of a faith in practice—the prayers, the prostrations. "But both methods lead to the same place," James explained.

We paid our bill and set off for the tent village on foot. Away from the stupa grounds, the streets were congested. Taxis swerved and honked to overtake each other, and uniformed kids stepped over downed wires and potholes on their way to school. On one corner, a construction project was underway. Three saronged women stood in flip-flops atop a dusty heap of gravel. One watered the pile with a battered hose, while the other two worked shovels to make cement. A bus rumbled by, leaving a wake of black soot.

I pulled my scarf up over my mouth. If it seemed like random chaos to me, James could see patterns in the scene. Through the din of the choked street, he pointed out a line of shoe-shiners squatting on crates. "Those men over there are drunks from the village."

A teenager appeared in front of us on the sidewalk, holding a Dutch coin in his outstretched hand. James pocketed the coin and handed over a rupee note. "I'm also known as a money changer around here."

We parted from the main street and turned down the trash-strewn alley that led to the village. We passed an old woman stooped under a huge basket of rutabagas. A man in a wheelchair bumped along behind her. "The King of Boudha!"—James called out. A million-dollar smile broke across the man's face.

The alley opened into an expanse of huts cobbled from bamboo and tarps. Children gathered around, reaching their small fingers up toward us. James shooed them away, scolding them for begging from his friends.

We found Puja washing aluminum dishware at a small spigot with a thin, soapy stream flowing behind her. She stood up, tossed her braid back, and repositioned her mustard-yellow sari. She flashed a shy ivory smile. With a little knowledge of English, Puja served as a sort of intermediary between James and the village. She greeted us and went for tea.

While Puja boiled water, James walked around the camp to exchange greetings. This community of 500 people began 25 years ago, when three Rajasthani families arrived in hopes of finding work near the touristy stupa. Things must have been desperate in Rajasthan, as the work-scene in Nepal is pretty dismal: with a 47-percent unemployment rate, those lucky enough to glean work can expect to labor for about $2.50 a day. But the village has managed to keep afloat with begging and shoe-shining for over two decades now.

And things are looking up since James helped start the quilt business. Now the women spend their days hand-stitching bright designs that sell for $150 each—enough to send their children to school for a year.

They regard James with great reverence. Just weeks ago, he appeared for one of his regular visits, and they pulled him by the arms to the corner of the village. There they'd built him his own hut—a tarp tent that granted the best view in the neighborhood: a sunny, tall grass field in a city where open space comes at a premium.

We ducked inside Jame's new place and waited for Puja to bring tea. The walls were decorated with posters of fruits and vegetables and images of Hindu deities.

James had to explain to the villagers that, though flattered, he was content in his apartment near the stupa. But he stocked his new village digs with tables and chairs and declared it a study room for the kids.

Puja came into the hut with a tray of scalding hot teas. "Puja makes the best tea," James said clasping one of the mug handles, "just the perfect amount of ginger." She closed her eyes and smiled.

We sipped our tea and mostly communicated in the universal language of smiles and nods.

Then James asked: "Puja, could you show us some quilts?"

She pulled one out of the dark corner and unfolded it, creating a shock of color against the dingy mud and tarp greens of the hut. Since the women scavenge leftover materials from tailor shops, they make do with what's available: pinks are combined with oranges, browns with reds. Lacking a quilting tradition, the women are unbound by conventional approaches, and the results are beautiful and artistic—the blanket perimeters are edged with fabric flowers, and the threads holding the pieces together vary in color and size.

If starting a quilt business out of scraps sounds straightforward, it hasn't been. In setting up the project, James had to contend not just with finding fabrics, setting up a website, and facilitating sales, but working with a totally different mindset.

Again and again with the village, James comes up against the double-edged sword of Nepali contentment. It's the national mood, embodied by the cliché *ke garne*, which means "What to do?" In the best sense, the phrase reflects an admirable acceptance of what can't be changed. But, at its worst, it indicates an apathy that has kept the country stuck and poor.

"The caste system means there is no pulling yourself up by the bootstraps. They have a different idea of success—a nicely different idea. Praying and having a big family is success."

James acknowledges these values but sees real problems in the areas of comfort, health, and sanitation. It's taken some work for the villagers to envision a better future and more secure life. He explains that they don't concern themselves with long-term planning. "They are understandably caught up in immediate needs. It's 'what's-for-lunch-right-now.'"

To counter this, he's started a savings program by giving them each their own box where he'll match whatever rupees they drop in. He's also convinced them of the importance of school, which is all about planning for the future.

On our way back to the stupa, we stopped in at the Kumari Sadan school. The principle came out from his office to greet us.

Achyut Prasad Pudasaini wore a navy blue jacket, gray trousers, and a neatly trimmed mustache. His stick-straight posture gave him an air of nobility that stood in stark contrast to the crumbling walls of the school. "Welcome!" he said with a slight bow. "Come. Please." He led us into an empty classroom. "We have 100 students total in this school. James has helped sponsor twenty-four of them!"

He turned and looked squarely at me: "Twenty-four! That's not a joke!"

The classroom was spartan: dingy concrete walls and metal benches. A weak shaft of light filtered through a tiny window. Drawings of flowers and rabbits were tacked near the cracked chalkboard. Up near the ceiling in large lettering, a quote: *If wealth is lost, nothing is lost. If health is lost everything is lost.*

"This school is in trouble," Principal Pudasaini confessed later, when we were drinking tea in his office, which doubles as a roughshod library for the children. The school opened in 1986 as a place where Kathmandu's poorest children could be educated.

"The government gives us no money," he told us. The school is under-stocked and understaffed, lacking books, computers, teachers. But there are even more fundamental needs: "You can see it's cold now, and the children don't have jackets."

Principal Pudasaini sees the connection between education and the fate of Nepal. "This country is very sweet. Very nice—like Switzerland! But there is a dirty game being played by the government. They are not clear-headed! We need real leaders for the future. Not just talkers!"

◆◆◆

I don't know if the Nepali are happier or not. As we traced our way back toward the stupa, passing trash heaps and skinny dogs, an image lingered in my mind:

Principal Pudasiani standing in the center of the drab "music room" with its crummy tape player and poor lighting, in his starched blue jacket and perfect posture, chin up. He'd been to America. He'd toured the great libraries of our colleges. He was well aware of what he did and didn't have to work with.

I can still see him now: extending his arms and issuing a declaration that sounded pessimistic, but might be just what Nepal needs: "I am not satisfied."

Nepali Elder
Photo by Molly McKissick

Writing on the playa in Yelapa with Laurie Wagner
Photo by Christina Ammon

PART TWO

Mexico

Deep Travel Mexico: The Art of Tranquilo

Each winter, Deep Travel hosts a writing retreat in the rugged-and-wonderful, car-free village of Yelapa on Mexico's Bay of Banderas. In this unpolished *paradiso* of sun, *cerveza*, and seafood, we find easy inspiration. After waking in our open-air *casitas*, we amble down the beach for a writing session and then enjoy the days sketching, swimming, hiking, boating—or all of the above! On our Yelapa trips, we do our best to balance rest and adventure. Want to sip margaritas in a hammock? Want to salsa dance in the moonlight? Want to enjoy Huichol art? How about fishing? Whatever we do there, we find plenty of inspiration for our journals.

Crossing the Beverage Barrier

NANCY KESSLER

It is said necessity is the mother of invention, but sometimes the spark of creativity is driven by want, such as in the desire for a drink.

And, you never know when or where the need will hit.

We are staying in Yelapa, a small, sunny, and warm *pueblo costera* (coastal town) in Mexico, *una ensenada* (cove) catering to tourists and my fellow writing workshop participants. Our hosts, Anna and Christina, kindly left us a bottle of *tequila reposato*, or aged tequila, and a bowlful of lovely, tiny, bright green, sweet and tangy limes in our room, knowing my sweetheart, workshop leader Tim Cahill, enjoys indulging in an after-work cocktail.

I, on the other hand, have a wary respect for the blue agave, earned many years ago, many, many miles north, in a place many, many degrees colder. That night, I met some girlfriends for a Christmas drink after a long week of work, needing only to finish packing for my trip to another snowy holiday destination before leaving on a 6 AM flight.

Our local *taverna, El Buho*, or The Owl, was often frequented by my friends for a drink called "The Fishbowl," a softball-sized and -shaped glass, which the infamous bartender Dana (but that's another story) would fill with ice and straight tequila, topped with a squeeze of lime.

I had never indulged in a Fishbowl, but Kelly and Gloria encouraged me to live large and kick off my vacation. And so I did, and did again, and again, and…. After five Fishbowls, I crawled home happy, packed my bag with alacrity, and crashed at 11 PM.

At 3 AM, I bolted upright in bed, wide awake, still past tipsy, and asked myself, "What the hell is in that suitcase?" I pulled it over, flung it open, and discovered that for my ten-day visit home, I had packed 23 sweaters, and not a single pair of socks.

Needless to say, I have limited my tequila-drinking ever since.

Tim knows I rarely drink liquor straight, so he kindly asks Mr. Google for some tequila beverage recipes—not margaritas—that we might easily make in our *casita* with ingredients found at the local *tienda*. Nothing quite fits the bill, nor can we find all the mixings at the store, so I improvise on the spot, picking this and that in hopes the blend would be potable.

Later that day, I try my newly invented cocktail, and find it to be not only *sabrosa, fresca, y refrescante*—tasty, cool, and refreshing—but good enough to deserve a real name and worldwide acclaim. Tim, too, finds it to his liking and helps devise the perfect moniker to celebrate the potion and the place.

We call it *Yelapa Sol.*

Herewith, fellow workshoppers, the recipe:

- Fill a tall glass with ice
- Add 1-2 shots of tequila (to taste)
- Fill the rest of glass with ½ Seven-Up and ½ *agua minerale* (club soda)
- Add squeeze of lime, stir and sip
- Repeat as desired

Feel free to share the formula, demand it at your local tavern, and help give it the fame it so tastily deserves. *A tu salud!*

Yelapa playa, Bay of Banderas
Photo by Tim Daw

Jackpot

RUBY TOOTSIE HANES

I watched in disbelief as the water taxi to Yelapa left Puerto Vallarta's Los Muertos pier without me. "Oh no," I groaned, "the last boat of the day!"

"No worry, *señora*," said an old fisherman looking up from his tackle box. "Not last boat. Another here very soon."

It arrived 20 minutes later. The flat-bottomed boat held 22 passengers facing forward on benches. As the only tourist, I was directed to sit in the rear for an easier ride. My suitcase was hurled under the deck.

The skipper aimed the boat at the sun perched high above a distant mountain. The craft skimmed lightly over the water, re-energizing my body and spirit. I'd been awake more than 35 hours.

During the ride, another water taxi buzzed alongside us. The boatmen eyed each other, and with a nod, full-throttled their engines. The front end of my boat reared like a stallion and slapped down so hard my teeth met my ass through my shoulders and spine.

While gripping the edge of my bench, a text from my friend, Christina, came through requesting my arrival time. I shouted the question to the captain. He yelled, "Another 45 minutes." Oh hell!

My anxiety increased as I recalled the unheeded advice

from my best friend. I'd argued, "I know I'm broke, but I need this trip. It's a writing retreat, and I need to reboot my skills."

"OK, but don't say you weren't warned."

It was dark when the boat finally idled up to Bahia Pier. Christina met me at the dock, her long hair swirling in the wind. She waved vigorously, her brow furrowed. She and two guys helped me disembark. "Watch your fingers," she said as the boat cracked against the old pier.

Day One: The Art of *Tranquilo*

Christina hauled my suitcase up jagged stairs to my private entrance at Casa Aña Rosa just behind the pier. I begged Strength to keep me upright.

After hugs Christina said, "I'll be right back to take you to dinner."

"OK!"

Scoping out my new digs, I paused in front of a mirror. Horror struck my eyes. Every single two-inch strand of hair on my head was extended full length. I looked like I stuck my finger in an electrical outlet. No wonder Christina frowned when she saw me.

I straightened myself up and settled my hair down. Christina returned and escorted me to dinner at The Yacht Club for Day One of the meet and greet. Nice place. I met everyone in my group including the facilitator, Dot Fisher-Smith.

Nearly a century old, an original tree-hugger who had trekked the Himalayas, she exclaimed "Here We Are NOW!! All of us!! Just imagine, we are here Now!!"

Weary and bleary, I had no patience for that. I knew it was NOW, dammit!

I ordered a bowl of tortilla soup to-go and retired to my

room. Thinking no more of the chatter, I settled in. My soup was delicious. All was well.

Day Two: *Ahora*

I remove my watch and put it back in my suitcase.
We're on Mexican time now.—Tony Cohan

Being in trip-recovery mode, I skipped the first workshop. Scoping my surrounds was my goal. No creepy-crawlers. I checked.

After a breakfast of vanilla-and-sugar pancakes at the Bahia Cafe, I went back to *mi casa* and met Señora Aña Rosa. When I told her it was my birthday, she sang Happy Birthday to me in Spanish. Her warmth stole my heart.

My friends, Brenda and Tim, soon arrived to show me around. We went shop-seeing and saw wonderful stuff. Later, we chose the *Taqueria Los Abuelos* near the *playita* to eat. At the *playita*, children played on old wooden boats. Dogs roamed freely.

A quiet sweetness prevailed as we absorbed exotic energy from soft tropical breezes, the sound of children at play, and the gentle lapping of the sea. Pure, unbridled joy crept through my being, now glistening in margaritas and fine company. In my heart of hearts, I thought I'd hit the jackpot of existence. Truly I did. Simple, quiet, and so very alive! *Tranquilo* indeed!

Later that night, the group met at *Tacos y Mas* for crazy-good fish tacos. One of the ladies offered to meet me the next day at my place to take me to Lagunitas for the next session. When I asked what I missed in the last session, Dot said, "Don't worry. Make-up is not required. Whatever comes up is what we do."

Day Three: *Caminos*

One is never really lost in Mexico. All streets lead to good
cantinas. All good stories start in cantinas.
—Rodolfo Anaya

The next day I overslept. Racing to meet my colleague, I
forgot the slip of paper with the workshop details. Worse,
she wasn't there. I had no clue where to go. Someone
suggested I call an ATV taxi to take me to the workshop. I
did. Soon, a young male driver showed up revving his
engines. "One hundred pesos."

"Fine! *Gracias.*"

An ATV holds three people on one super-sized bicycle
seat: the driver straddles the front, and two people sit behind
him. Another person can sit on the front fender if they don't
mind having nothing to hold onto.

"Back seat, back seat." he said.

Did he think I was going to ride in the front?

Unaided, I hoisted myself up. The seat fit like a side-
saddle of sorts—one leg dangled while I braced myself with
the other on the fender. I held tight to a thin tube of chrome
across the back of the ATV.

Up the hill we went, making a sharp right turn and
hugging a high white stucco wall that had *Fuck You* written
across it. We whisked past doorways that opened into family
homes. Then up, up, up, windier and more bouncy until the
road entered the jungle. Ten minutes later, he stopped the
vehicle abruptly and jumped off. *Did I give him wrong*
information? Was he out of gas?

He pushed the ATV around the tight left turn and then
got back on.

A wide, shallow, brown river stretched before us. We
were going in. I sucked in my breath and held on. Water
splashed up my legs. *Indiana Jones you have nothing on me.*

A road popped up at the opposite side of the river. A few minutes later, we were at my destination. The driver stopped the vehicle and held out his hand. *"Aqui!"*

"Are you sure?" I said climbing down unassisted and handing over the pesos. Looking around, I saw no one. I turned, paused, scanned, circled, paused, scanned, circled. *Someone? Anyone? No one!* It was mid-morning. The tables under the *palapas* were empty.

Confused, I foot-slogged through coarse, deep, coral-colored sand all the way to the other end of the beach, looking fruitlessly for my group. Finally, I retraced my steps and found an ATV to take me back to *mi casa* where I flopped down on my comfy day bed with my legs elevated. I watched coconut trees sway in the breeze against the brilliant sky. Sounds from the sea lullabied me to sleep. Missing the workshop mattered not.

Later, feeling refreshed, I explored my outside surroundings. Uneven shrubs of yellow and pink flowers flanked edges of a path which became a delightful short-cut to a restaurant where dinner was planned that evening.

After dinner, a huge bonfire at the beach topped off the day.

Day Four: *Colores*

"In nature, colors never clash."
The same can be said of Mexico.
—Jeff Greenwald quoting Allan Becker

After breakfast with friends, I managed to make it to the session on time. Curiously, the spot seemed to be right by the ATV drop-off point where I'd arrived the day before.

The workshop started without pre-theming the discussion. As people spoke, I couldn't find my place in what was going on. It felt like a 12-step program without the steps. One finely tuned-in businesswoman shared her biggest fear, and that was to die with a guilty conscience. This workshop was not what I expected.

I remained disconnected and wondered what was here that I needed to know. Still, in the after-glow of good times, I blurted out the only thing that came to mind and that was, "How does one know when they hit the so-called jackpot?"

Blank looks met my words. I pushed. "No, really, how do you know?" Throats cleared. Some left for the bathroom. The conversation moved on without me.

Day Five: *Junto*

Each of us is born with a box of matches inside us
but we can't strike them all by ourselves.
—Laura Esquivel, *Like Water for Chocolate*

I made it to the next workshop in time and without a fuss. Again, out of nowhere, the session began. A very professional, well-seasoned woman pitched about how badly she felt when her guitar was stolen—practically under her eyes. Now she was in the market for a gun. Yikes. No fun here. I tried to offer some wisdom, but it went flat. Thankfully, the session ended and we moved onto food and shopping. We were on our own for lunch.

That evening, the group met at Garcia's Rentals to hike to Manguitos, a restaurant on a hiking trail that ultimately led to a waterfall. Glad I wore my hiking boots.

It was my birthday, and so I was placed at the head of the table. My margarita was fabulous and so was my salad and mountain of barbecued shrimp. Somehow, I ended up with two margaritas. A person put a birthday cupcake in front of me with a firecracker in it. I watched in awe as it lit the table and popped overhead, spraying sparkles as it drifted down. Breathtaking! Then the party was over and I was ushered to a waiting ATV taxi by a husband and wife team that was anchored by my side. I had hardly finished my salad.

Day Six: The Day Time Forgot

I spent my last day in great physical discomfort. In bed, the room swirled. Montezuma's revenge hit fast and hard. Señora Aña Rosa provided bananas and Gatorade to ease my condition, but it was the many Imodiums I swallowed later that saved my beleaguered ass.

I slept fitfully that night and woke early on day seven for my return trip home. After squeezing into an over-stuffed boat, heavy with more than 22 passengers, I offered silent thanks for the silky-smooth ride back to Vallarta.

It took more than a month to recuperate from the journey. Even though I took this trip to refine my writing skills, I learned something more important. To achieve a feeling of tranquility in the midst of chaos, it's best to be in a tropical paradise.

After deep reflection on motives and lessons from this trip, I have come to realize that whether I am filled with joy, fear, or doubt, I am in the right place at the right time, all the time, performing the right actions.

Jackpot? Maybe!

Getting Underground in Mexico's Maya Riviera

JACQUELINE YAU

"The caves are a gateway to the underworld," said Rio Secreto guide Pablo Salce Zambrano as our group of eight travelers prepared to descend into a series of caverns beneath the Maya Riviera on Mexico's Yucatan Peninsula. "When you go down, you die," he said, pausing, "and then (when you emerge from the caves) you get reborn."

I'd hesitated when cousins suggested my husband and I join them on a tour of Rio Secreto. I had visions of an overly bright, bleached-out cavern with a bunch of stalactites hanging from the ceiling, nothing I hadn't seen before. I felt that visiting a cave was probably going to contribute to its degradation, and when Pablo started talking about dying, that conjured new concerns. But we were intrigued by what lay beneath the surface and wanted to share the adventure with family, so we decided to take the plunge and go.

The Rio Secreto guides were eager to protect the underground caverns and the water that flows through them, asking all guests to shower off any sunscreen and hair products that could contaminate the Secret River. "Our job is to preserve this place," Pablo said.

The caves were discovered in the 1990s on privately held

land; more than 10 miles of caverns had been mapped when we visited in 2009. The Rio Secreto tour only covers about 700 yards, but detours into side passages and sloshing through the water makes it feel longer.

The tour followed a rope line through waterways in the inky darkness. Rio Secreto, near Playa del Carmen, about 50 miles south of Cancun, is draped with so many natural wonders it almost seemed like it was designed by the Disney animators who created *Fantasia*. It turned out to be the ideal way to get underground in this limestone-rich region.

We got into wetsuits and life-jackets, then dropped into a nondescript entrance, just a small space between some shrubs, that gave no hint of what lay below. At the entrance, we were greeted by a Mayan altar with candles and totems.

The yellow beam of my headlamp bounced off the icicle-shaped stalactites daggering the ceiling of the cavern as I waded into clear, blue-green water. Artful lighting—in bright blue, orange, and red—highlighted the natural cathedral of stalactites and stalagmites around us. The water was "*fresca* not *fria*" Pablo said, then he quickly returned to English: cool not cold.

We learned to read the structures as we walked, waded, and swam through the ancient spaces. Pablo gave us a quick lesson about how the caves and stalactites and stalagmites are formed. In brief, erosion of the soft limestone creates the caverns: the 'tites and 'mites grow from thousands of years of drips that leave infinitesimal amounts of minerals behind.

Above us was a natural chandelier, white with age. A bat flitted over my head, flying by an orange-tinged stalagmite. Blue revealed manganese in the stalactite flag sculpture. Some dripstones looked like a wavy curtain, perhaps indicating that a slight breeze had somehow sneaked in, shaping the structures little by little.

When we reached a cavernous room, deep inside Rio Secreto, Pablo had us all sit down in the water. He turned off the light—we found ourselves wrapped in silence and impenetrable darkness. As the first few minutes passed, I wondered what would happen if none of our lights came back on. Becoming a sacrifice to the Mayan gods crossed my mind, but I snapped into the present and just relaxed into the experience, feeling calm and peace wash down over me. Normally, I'm afraid of the dark but I wasn't scared. The absence of sight and sound in this space felt expansive and freeing. We were bound together in sacred stillness. "Leave your worries behind," Pablo said; the cave can hold them.

As soon as Pablo turned his flashlight on, a tiny moth fluttered by—a sign that fresh air was near. We followed the rope line until the odorless cave dramatically gave way to the earthy scent of the living world. We saw a speckle of light up ahead and ascended, soon trampling over deadened leaves ground into dirt instead of limestone. The world seemed greener, bluer, and so much brighter, more vibrant. I emerged with gratitude and harmony in my heart for experiencing this hallowed place.

Though I had moments of trepidation, I never felt the Rio Secreto tour was risky. Rather, it was one of many ways to get beneath the surface of Mexico's Yucatan Peninsula, a pursuit that revealed slices of the place that most visitors don't see. Experiencing this bit of unexpected paradise with family left me feeling immense appreciation.

Beyond the wondrous caves are cenotes, natural pools formed by the collapse of limestone, creating sinkholes that fill with water and become oases for swimming or snorkeling. Our experience at Rio Secreto whetted our appetite to explore more of the watery oases in this region. In parts of the Yucatan, cenotes are linked by creeks so you can paddle a kayak from one to the next, then jump out and take a swim or snorkel. No trip to the Yucatan is complete without a dip in a cenote.

My husband and I took a dip at Cenote Ik Kil, the sacred

blue cenote, located at the eco-archeological park Ik Kil, in the interior of the Yucatan, about three miles away from the Mayan ruins of Chichen Itza. From a height of about 85 feet, I could see down the giant circular, well-like hole, into the clear blue water below. Skeins of tree roots, vines, palm fronds, and other lush vegetation tumbled over the opening and dropped straight down into the cenote, framing a waterfall streaming down. A shaft of sunlight made the falling droplets dance in the sun and spotlighted swimmers as they dog-paddled among schools of fish.

Along the sides of the cenote, sheer limestone walls rose up and up. We descended the grand, stone, spiral staircase. I climbed down a wooden ladder and splashed into the cenote. Bliss. Cenotes, fed by crystal-clear underground rivers, are refreshing and bracing, the ultimate antidote to a hot, sticky day. I floated under the waterfall and closed my eyes under the beam of sunlight. When I popped back up, I saw fish swimming below me. Then I swam from one end of the 200-foot wide pool to the other. The bottom appeared fathomless, but I knew it was 130 feet deep.

Going to one cenote just sparked our interest to explore more. At Hacienda Tres Ríos, an eco-resort just south of Playa del Carmen, we biked to about seven different cenotes and snorkeled in one that flowed out to the ocean. The water was so clear that the shadow of my body reflected onto the rocks below. As I swam, memories of delightful childhood adventures tromping through parks and exploring the denizens of lakes near my home tumbled over me. I had that same magical feeling of discovery I experienced as a child. We followed black-striped yellow fish down the current, floating past fallen trees, roots, and algae then kayaked along the cenote river as a family of coatis, which look like the offspring of a raccoon and an anteater, followed alongside on the branches of the mangroves. My amateur paddling startled a flock of snowy egrets, which fanned out, only to circle and land back onto a large mangrove tree.

As Mayan legends suggest, rising from the depths gave us a sense of renewal. Our journey to Rio Secreto left me feeling at peace and in harmony with the environment. And we emerged from our all-too-brief swim through the Yucatan's cenotes rejuvenated and refreshed, ready for whatever lay ahead.

This story was first published by *Inspirato* magazine.

The jungles of Riviera Nayarit
Photo by Tree Knowlton

Las Palmas

ABBY FRINK

I heard unearthly screaming in the night. It came from across the river.

Hushed voices the next day. "Juan Carlos," they said, "you know, the guy who climbed the *palmas* and got the coconuts? Juan Carlos."

As I walked around to the beach that morning, a vigil had formed outside his house, where the body still lay. Where his wife and three children had found him hanging from a rope.

"It was the crystal," they said, "he couldn't quit it."

A procession brought the casket to the church in town later that same day. No funeral parlor or preparing the body. The reality of a small town in a warm climate.

The casket was placed just outside the church doors. Juan Carlos was not allowed to enter. His choice to die not permitted by his church. Family and friends stood outside with him, keeping him company in his banishment.

My friend motioned for me to join her as a procession formed to lead the casket up the steep steps and dirt path to the crowded cemetery on the edge of town. There among plastic-covered pictures of virgins and saints, faded artificial flowers and votive candles, stood the graves of the town's deceased. Friends of Juan Carlos had spent the day digging his grave. They sat with shovels in hand, dirty, sweaty, and drunk with their legs dangling into the grave.

I stood and watched as the townspeople trudged up that steep hill. Young and old, friends and enemies, to pay tribute to Juan Carlos.

I watched as his wife screamed in grief and his little girls looked on in horror as they lowered him into the grave.

I watched as a community came together to take care of its own in death. And I wondered, now, who among those gathered would climb the *palmas* and get the coconuts?

The Ghosts of Alamos

LAVINIA SPALDING

The sun is relentless, stalking me along the narrow, cobbled lanes of Alamos, Mexico, as I return to my hotel. I unlock the heavy double doors and walk into the lush, untamed courtyard, where weather-pocked stone cherubs guard a center fountain and rocking chairs sit motionless beneath electric ceiling fans. It's quiet inside. Quieter, in fact, than any hotel I've ever patronized, because I'm the only guest.

Which is not to say that I'm alone.

According to locals, my hotel is haunted by the woman it originally belonged to: Señorita Marcor, a beautiful spinster piano teacher who traversed Alamos only by underground tunnel because the streets back then weren't cobbled, and she refused to muddy her boots and long skirts.

This doesn't alarm me. For one thing, I like the sound of Señorita Marcor. For another, I'm traveling with my own ghost.

"I want to disappear," I told my mother a few weeks ago, giving her a research project. My father had just died, so I thought she could benefit from an assignment that would keep her busy, give her a purpose. As for me, I was desperate to escape San Francisco—the endless hustle, the cold summer weather, the impassive faces, and worse, the sympathetic ones. I wanted to retreat with my memories of my father to a place where no one knew us.

"Maybe Mexico," I said. "Somewhere pretty but not touristy—a quiet village with a couple of small hotels and coffee shops. And bougainvillea. Lots of bougainvillea."

It took her two days to return a verdict: Alamos, a seventeenth-century colonial town in the foothills of the Sierra Madres, one of Mexico's oldest treasures and a national monument. A tourist destination in the winter, it would be disgustingly hot and accordingly devoid of visitors in June. I could take a first-class, air-conditioned bus from Tucson—where she lived—leaving at 6:00 PM and arriving at 6:00 AM, for $80 round-trip.

"Alamos," I said, rolling it on my tongue like a Mexican candy. "I've never heard of it. Sounds perfect."

◆ ◆ ◆

When I step off the bus at 6:00 AM, however, I'm less convinced. It's quiet here, all right. The sun is just beginning its rise, exposing thin, dusty streets surrounding the station. Lifeless and bleak, they don't promise much—no bougainvillea, no inviting B&Bs, and not a single coffee shop brightens the pale, nondescript rows of single-story dwellings. Of the few local characters lurking about, none speak English, and I'm struggling with Spanish. I have only a few key words in my arsenal, and I'm hoping if I can put them in the right order, they'll lead me to caffeine.

"*Restaurante?*" I inquire of the driver. He's leaning against the bus, pinching a cigarette tightly between his thumb and forefinger. No, he assures me, shaking his head once, definitively. No *restaurantes*. All closed at this hour.

So I camp out at the station and wait for the town to open its doors to me, miserably watching the ticket agent sip coffee from a thermos. Wishing I knew enough Spanish to engineer a transaction that would result in my getting a cup.

Wishing I had pesos to offer. Wishing I knew the whereabouts of my formerly travel-savvy, super badass self.

Finally around 7:30, I strike out, following twisty cobbled roads into the center of town. For some reason, the sidewalks in Alamos are elevated a good three feet from the ground—almost shoulder height for me. Unsure of what to make of this, I instead walk in the road, which means each time a little pickup blows through, I'm forced to press against the wall of the sidewalk to make room for both of us.

Within minutes my enthusiasm returns as I find myself surrounded by bright white Spanish colonial architecture, completely intact, and endless rows of tall, arched portals. I'm relieved by the absence of fast-food restaurants and scant suggestions of Western influence. No one is hawking blankets or tacky mother-of-pearl jewelry, or sipping Starbucks lattes while barking into cell phones. I see only a handful of locals beating dust from rugs, opening windows, calmly sweeping sidewalks. They cast shy looks my way, and something about them restores my confidence.

Soon I find myself at Casa de los Tesoros, a sixteenth-century convent turned tourist hotel. I spend the morning there, drinking Nescafé and nibbling on thick Mexican pastries delivered by clean-shaven servers in suits and ties. The manicured courtyard has café tables with umbrellas, a gift shop, a swimming pool, and an Internet station set up beneath massive, ancient-looking paintings of monks and saints.

Within an hour I've committed the very act I swore I wouldn't—I've made a friend: Jean-Philippe, a Parisian toy designer who came here to purchase a million jumping beans to sell in the pages of French magazines. Alamos, he informs me, is the jumping-bean capital of the world.

"Only, for the first time since 1982," he says, his face darkening, "they aren't jumping. The rain came too early this year, ruining the chances for a crop."

But he's solved the problem, he announces, turning cheerful again as he reaches for one of my pastries. He's invented a cardboard chicken that lays real, edible square eggs. This is exactly the sort of bizarre conversation I usually relish when traveling, but today it feels misplaced. I'm not in Mexico to make friends or conversation or be served poolside by well-coifed waiters. I'm not here to have a good time. I'm here for one reason: to lean into grief till I fall over and have no choice but to pull myself back up again.

My immediate problem is solved when I meet Suzanne, the owner of Casa de los Tesoros. After a brief conversation in which I explain that I'm a writer in search of simpler, quieter lodging (no need to tell anyone about my father), I find myself being led to her other hotel down the road where, if I stay, I'll be the sole occupant.

From the outside, Hotel la Mansion appears stark and pedestrian, and I brace myself to meet the dumpy little sister of Casa de los Tesoros. But Suzanne casually unlocks the heavy double doors, and I step past her into a wild, tropical, secret-garden-like courtyard. A central stone fountain bubbles, surrounded by palm and mango trees, white pillars and statues. Slanted beams of sunlight illuminate thick curls of pink bougainvillea hanging from white arches, and birds circle the tops of trees. Hummingbirds buzz and pale yellow butterflies flutter, and it feels like the doors have been sealed for a century. Suzanne offers me my choice of ten rooms, and then she closes the gate behind her.

My father would have been thrilled that I've come to Mexico to mourn him; he loved Latin American and Spanish culture. He collected Day of the Dead statues, Tarahumara pottery, and Mexican postcards of 1930s film stars; he devoured everything he could find to read about pre-Columbian history, the Mayans, the mummies of Guanajuato. But mostly he loved the music. A concert classical and flamenco guitarist, he studied in Mexico with

Manuel Lopez Ramos and in Spain with Paco de Lucía, and he once performed at the palace of Alfonso the XIII for the Prince of Spain. And when he was diagnosed with terminal emphysema and advised that he could buy himself six more months by moving to a lower elevation, my father immediately chose Tucson—he wanted to go to the Mariachi Festival.

◆◆◆

I spend my first Alamos afternoon in one of the old Mother Hubbard rocking chairs outside my room, reading and writing in my journal. Finally, around dusk, I venture out to find food. In the town square I buy a book called *See It and Say It in Spanish* from a woman named Marta at Terracotta Tiendas, a co-op in the plaza, and study it over a bowl of tortilla soup and a Corona at Las Palmeras, a quiet, low-key restaurant across from the plaza.

Directly in front of me stands the centerpiece of town, a gloomy, shadowy church called Iglesia de Nuestra Señora de la Concepción or La Parroquia de la Purisima Concepción or El Templo Parroquial de la Immaculada Concepción, depending on whom you ask. And right in front of the church, as if to cheer it up, is the Plaza de las Armas, with a delicate open-sided gazebo surrounded by flowers, a smattering of gangly skyscraper palm trees, and a wrought iron and white picket fence.

Like its church, Alamos has multiple names—the City of Arches, the Flower of the North, the Pearl of the Mountains, the Garden of the Gods, the City of Silver, and the Soul of the Sierra Madre—but Francisco de Vasquez Coronado first named it Alamos (or Real de Los Frailes de Alamos) in 1540. The northernmost of Mexican colonial cities, it became one of the wealthiest towns in the country after silver was discovered in the hills in 1683. By the late 1700s, the town had more than 30,000 residents, some of whom traveled north to found San Francisco and Los Angeles.

By 1790, Alamos was one of the world's biggest silver producers and by the mid-nineteenth century, the capital of Occidente. But with riches came trouble; for two centuries, the people of Alamos suffered floods, droughts, plagues, and famine along with political unrest and continual Apache, Yaqui, Mayo and Tarahumara uprisings. Colonists, Federalists, Liberals, and bandits overran the town at one time or another. In the 1860s, under Napoleon's reign, Emperor Maximilian's troops occupied Alamos and drove away all the silver barons. Mexican rebels took it back the following year, and the Revolution drove away most colonial landowners. By the early 1900s, the mines were closed, along with the railroad and the mint. The money was gone, and only a few hundred people remained.

But it still held some magic, because the story goes that when Pancho Villa's troops arrived in Alamos in 1915, intending to pillage the town, he gave orders to not burn it, vowing to someday make it his home. Villa was killed shortly after, so he never returned. Instead, after World War II, Americans began immigrating and restoring the old adobe mansions. Now Alamos is a national monument, with 188 buildings on the national registry, and it's home to some 15,000 people, including about 400 expats (Paul Newman, Carroll O'Connor, Rip Torn, Gene Autry, and Roy Rogers all lived here). Still, it doesn't feel like an expat town.

◆ ◆ ◆

From the window of Las Palmeras, I watch people mill about the Plaza de las Armas, settling into benches around the church and gazebo. Two handsome old mustached men in matching cowboy hats lean cross-armed against the ornate white fence that frames the gazebo, and behind them, a teenage couple holds hands shyly in the shade of a jacaranda tree. A woman sets up a *hamborgesa* stand, and a man carries a guitar case across the plaza.

My father was teaching guitar right up until he died, still patiently explaining to his students how to do a tremolo or a *rasgueado*, jiggling their wrists to make them relax their hands, scolding them for hooking their thumbs over the necks of their guitars.

I studied seriously with him from when I was five until thirteen, and again in my twenties and thirties, less seriously. Now that he's gone—and with him the opportunity to study—I'm already lost in regret for a lifetime of taking him for granted. It's not a surprise. I knew I'd feel remorse; I just didn't anticipate being so mad at myself.

My father left his guitar to me, but since he died, I've only removed it from its case a handful of times. I've held it in my arms, rested my cheek against the cool wood, played a few notes, and put it back. But suddenly I find myself wishing I'd brought it to Mexico. Perhaps here, in the haven of my hotel, I could make it through an entire piece of music.

The day he told me he was dying, I laughed at him.

"Dad, you're not dying," I said.

"Yes, I am. I have emphysema."

"A doctor told you that?"

"No."

"Then how do you know?" I asked.

"I Googled it."

I told him he was silly, but Google was right. His health declined over the next two years; he coughed and wheezed constantly, eventually barely able to breathe. Finally, he was put on an oxygen machine, which he dragged around the house with him. He quit smoking, reluctantly, after forty-five years.

The last time I talked to him, I was in a rush to get off the phone. I had fifteen spare minutes before I needed to leave for work, but trying to carry on a conversation with him had turned painful; he was too often incoherent and rambled on.

"I've got to go, Daddy," I said.

"Well," he answered lightly, "when you gotta go, you gotta go."

The words stay with me.

◆ ◆ ◆

The Plaza de las Armas is quiet tonight, but not so on Sunday evenings, when the age-old ritual of *paseo* is still practiced, as it is in virtually every small town in Mexico: teenage boys and girls promenading, walking in circles around the gazebo in opposite directions, eyeing each other openly. It reminds me of high school weekends spent at the shopping mall, except the laps these teens make around each other are much shorter, and the prowling more overt.

But the true distinction is the parents, sitting on sideline benches taking in the entertainment of their daughters walking arm-in-arm with girlfriends, being ogled by pubescent boys. I think of what Suzanne said about my hotel's ghost, Señorita Marcor—that she had dozens of suitors but never married because her parents didn't approve of any of them.

Maybe little has changed since Señorita Marcor's day, and parents still preside over their children's love lives here. I consider the scene in front of me. It's fairly self-explanatory, but for one thing: I see no pairing off, no conversation or flirtation between the sexes. What comes next for these teens loosely upholding the culture's dating traditions? Will they date? Get married? And if their parents disapprove, will they run off and elope as my parents did?

My mother first met my father at her art school graduation party in Boston when she was 23 and he was 17.

"That's the cutest boy I've ever seen," she said to a friend when my father walked in with his guitar, crashing the party. "I'm going to marry him."

"I'd better introduce you, then," the friend said, ushering her over to him.

"Wally, meet Dolly," the introduction went. "You're made for each other."

Six weeks later they stole my aunt's car and ran off together, making it all the way to California. When they finally ran out of money, they called my grandmother and told her they'd eloped (they hadn't, but pretending to be married meant they could cohabitate). The following June they drove a borrowed TR3 sports car from Boston to North Carolina, where it was legal to marry at the age of 18 without parental consent. This time they actually did elope.

Before my father got sick, he was the star of the family, the vibrant, handsome, brilliant performer, and we orbited his life, for better or for worse, like these kids circumambulate the gazebo in Plaza de las Armas.

If the gazebo wasn't here, would they still walk the *paseo* every night? What do we do with the traditions and patterns when our center is suddenly gone?

◆ ◆ ◆

During the day not a soul visits my hotel, and I sit and listen to mangos drop from trees. I drink coffee, write, read, study Spanish, and nap. Sometimes I cry. Time spreads, expands.

But for a few hours each evening, Ruben, a worker from Casa de los Tesoros, comes by in case I need anything. Twenty-two and bored, Ruben likes to bring things to my door. First, chips and salsa. Next, bottled water. Finally, a mango from the tree outside my door. I'm determined to be alone, but he doesn't know that, and his earnestness makes it impossible to resent the interruptions. *Gracias*, I say, again and again. *Gracias.*

An elderly security guard also comes at night. He sits on a chair just inside the main door, though to protect me from what, I have no idea. I can only imagine it's the town ghosts, for I've come to learn that Señorita Marcos is not alone; legend has it Alamos is teeming with them. There's the gray-robed monk who guards the treasures in the seven secret underground tunnels leading to the church, the ghosts of the silver mine workers, the politically incorrect "headless Chinaman," the unfaithful bride, and the violet perfume ghost.

I find being in a ghost town soothes me. There's something about the way the people of Alamos so effortlessly preserve their past and coexist with their ghosts. I start leaving my hotel more frequently during the day, retreating to my air-conditioned room only when I get overheated. I strike up conversations with locals just to ask them about ghosts. Everyone has a story. In this town, spirits aren't a concept one does or does not believe in; they simply exist, almost as lively a populace as the living.

◆ ◆ ◆

Out wandering one day, I poke my head into Casa de Maria Felix, a hotel and museum. One of Alamos's claims to fame is that it's the birthplace of Maria Felix, an iconic film star sometimes referred to as the Mexican Marilyn Monroe. This is the property where she was born. It's run by an expat named Lynda, who tells me she was unaware, when she bought it in 1999, that the film star was born there.

She was not, however, oblivious to Maria Felix's existence. Coincidentally, she'd been collecting photos of the Mexican film star for thirty years. The casa now overflows with artifacts excavated during the construction of the hotel, and a room dedicated to images of Maria Felix runs the gamut from famous original portraits to what resemble middle-school art class sketches. Altogether, Lynda has some 400 images of Maria Felix.

Lynda's ghost story is that she came upon the ruin one night while taking a walk, during her first visit to Alamos. The moon was shining through a window, and behind the wall she could see mesquites and Palo Verde trees. Intrigued, she wandered to the back of the property and, turning to look at the ruins in the moonlight, saw the spirits of a woman and child. She bought the property the next day.

Later in the afternoon, I take a private walking tour with a man named Trini, who goes by Candy Joe (local kids gave him the moniker, he tells me, because he always has candy for them). We visit the cemetery, a study in shades of white and sepia. Elaborately carved statues of praying angels and weeping cherubs share sky space with towering, austere crosses, while beautiful old headstones are stacked on the ground like dishes in a cupboard. On one end of the graveyard, a tall block of aboveground family crypts all bear holes the size of grapefruits, evidence of a time when looting was standard practice.

Candy Joe also takes me by a mansion where a woman named Beatrice, a silver baron's daughter, once lived. The house was a wedding gift from Beatrice's father, he says. On the day she married, her father had the streets of Alamos lined with silver bars for a few hours. Leaving the church after the ceremony, though, the groom's horse was spooked and reared up; the groom was thrown and his back broken, and several months later he died. Beatrice subsequently lost her mind, and for the next six months could be spotted in the cemetery late at night, digging up his grave with a shovel and pick. Because her father was the most important man in town, the cemetery caretaker left her alone. She died not long after and was buried beside her husband, but people continued to see her ghost, in front of his grave, praying.

I find that the stories all intersect, weaving around each

other, cross-pollinating. Is it the virgin bride, the woman in white, or the unfaithful wife who haunts the beautiful mansion they call Las Delicias? Or are these spirits one and the same? The legends are fused, details blurred. They have been repeated so many times.

◆◆◆

The night before I leave Alamos, I have dinner with Suzanne, Jean-Philippe, and a few other travelers. As we swap stories, I realize that for the first time, I'm not eyeing the door, waiting for a break in conversation so I can escape. I'm content in the company of others. I even talk about my father.

For a place I hadn't heard of a month ago, Alamos has given me precisely what I wanted—gentle quietude and privacy, solitude without isolation, uninterrupted time and space to heal, no one asking anything of me. A summer season so slow and lazy that even the jumping beans won't jump, so hot and muggy it holds no appeal to any other tourists.

It's also provided what I didn't want but somehow needed. When I walk through town now, I know people. Jose Louis, the bartender at Casa de los Tesoros, is teaching me to conjugate verbs, Lynda from Casa Maria Felix has given me a driving tour, Candy Joe hollers *"Buenos dias"* from his little tourist office, and Marta from the co-op waves exuberantly whenever she sees me.

I came here to be alone in my grief, but it's the people of Alamos who have helped me move beyond it. Without even trying, they've taught me to remember the dead in a way that keeps them alive—by continuing to tell their stories.

This story won a Gold Solas Award & was previously published in *Gadling* & *The Best Travel Writing, Vol. 9* (Travelers' Tales, 2012).

Photo by Tim Daw

Tulum: Coastside Abode of the Gods

MICHAEL SHAPIRO

A Caribbean salsa band plays up-tempo Cuban songs as dozens of people dance on the beach below. On an open-air patio, Jackie and I feast on ultra-fresh ceviche and potent Herradura margaritas under the moonlight. This may sound like a scene from any number of Mexican beaches, but there's one big difference: we're swaying in the shadow of the Mayan ruins of Tulum.

This gleaming city on a hill, built eight centuries ago to give the local Mayans a commanding view of the sea, remains one of Mexico's most beguiling sights. Most Mayan ruins are inland, concealed by their jungle surroundings. Tulum occupies a blufftop and has a sunrise view overlooking the turquoise waters of the Caribbean Sea. And Tulum shows off the Mayans' flair for stone carvings, with figures of jaguars, fertility goddesses, and plumed serpents that evoke the resplendent quetzal, a bird that Maya leaders revered as an embodiment of spirit.

After a week on the Mayan Riviera in typical resorts near Cancun, Jackie (then my girlfriend and now my wife) and I sought a more down-to-earth Mexican experience. We wanted a place where beach sand didn't have to be trucked in, where Mayan ruins were just 10 minutes away, and where sea turtles had the right of way.

We found our paradise in Tulum, one of the most picturesque beachside resorts in the Yucatán. Less than two hours south of the Cancun airport, Tulum is everything that the growing resortopolis of Cancun is not: tranquil, lightly and thoughtfully developed, and home to Mayan ruins that almost appear to be hovering above the beach. Tulum has all the comforts one needs, but unlike in Cancun, you feel like you're in Mexico.

We arrived in Tulum without reservations not realizing it was the first Saturday of spring break week. (That was this savvy travel writer's idea: "Let's just look at a few places and pick one we really like." An hour into the search his loyal companion was not amused.) Jackie and I visited several lodges before we found our home for the weekend: a beachfront cabana on stilts about 25 yards from the lapping waves at Hotel Nueva Vida de Ramiro.

The light-tan sand felt as fine as baby powder; the water segued from cobalt blue to emerald green; the vibe was relaxed. Occasionally a vendor would stroll by offering hand-carved coral bracelets or homemade necklaces. The pieces were beautiful and the sell was as soft as the sand.

Hotel Nueva Vida is part of Tulum's Zona Hotelera, which stretches for several miles along the coast and is strictly regulated to prevent skyscrapers and haphazard development. Judging from the low-slung skyline, it seemed like no hotel in Tulum was taller than the highest palm tree, and most weren't half that high.

Which is not to say that Tulum isn't growing. When we visited in 2009, it was booming and certainly has grown since them. But growth should be limited by strict environmental regulations to maintain the delicate balance of nature, said Santiago Kenny, a young man who's part of the family that owns Hotel Nueva Vida.

The cabanas are built on stilts to prevent erosion, Kenny said, and the fence enclosing the cluster of bungalows was designed so baby sea turtles can crawl between the slats and get back to the ocean. During spawning season, the gate is left open so mother turtles can enter the property's sands. The hotel's white lights are replaced with dim red lamps so that the baby loggerheads and green turtles, which navigate by moonlight, don't get disoriented.

Our first night in the cabana, the sound of gently breaking waves lulled us to sleep. The next day we rose early (to beat the heat and the tour-bus crowds) and visited Tulum's Mayan ruins. We parked and walked about 10 minutes (just over half a mile) to the main entrance. Our jaws dropped when we reached the place where Tulum meets the sea. There are more spectacular Mayan ruins, but none in a more spectacular setting.

Late post-Classic period (13th-16th centuries) Mayan formations dominated the coastline, towering above the beach and limpid sea below. Some visitors descended the trail to loll on the sand, swim in the ocean, or cool off in a cenote (limestone pool) below the ruins. Archeologists believe Tulum was a port and military post, explaining its proximity to sea. When Spanish explorers "discovered" the walled city in 1518, they found stone buildings painted red, blue and gold. With walls several feet thick, it's clear Tulum was purpose-built as a fortress.

"Tulum" is a Mayan word for wall, though its residents called the city "Zama" meaning dawn, probably because Tulum is perfectly placed for viewing the sunrise. Walking through Tulum's ruins is a bit like navigating an IKEA store—you're supposed to follow a set route. After entering through a break in a long stone wall, you come to the Templo del Dios del Viento (Temple of the Wind Gods), a stone edifice built on a rocky outcropping with excellent views of El Castillo.

Named by the invading Spaniards, the imposing El Castillo is Tulum's icon: the stone fortress on a cliff jutting into the Caribbean Sea has figures of Toltec plumed serpents. As we passed by, several portly iguanas lumbered through the grounds and sunned themselves on the rocks.

At the 15th-century Templo de las Pinturas, a guide said the Maya used an insect called a *cochina* to produce red dye used to paint Tulum's facades. One human figure at the temple was painted with one eye open to show the duality between light and dark. The entry to the temple was so low even the stout Maya had to duck—the guide said that may have been a gesture of reverence to the goddess of fertility.

Outside Tulum several Mayan men were enacting a centuries-old tradition of swinging in circles around a towering pole on long ropes. Called the *palo volador,* the ritual featured four men in monkey costumes hitched by long lines to the top of the pole and "flying" 60 feet above the ground. From the ruins we drove into Tulum *pueblo* (the city side of Tulum along the main highway) and filled up on fresh fish tacos at a gritty roadside stand. Then it was back to our cabana for a lazy afternoon on the beach.

We'd allowed only two days for Tulum, but gazing at the hammock on our deck and the beach beyond made the thought of leaving unbearable, so we booked one more night. That would mean a dreadfully early airport departure the next day, but we didn't mind. As we sipped our margaritas and swayed to the live salsa music at La Zebra on our final night, time seemed to evaporate. We were blissfully happy; all that mattered was the moment, and the rest of the world, with all its demands, felt infinitely far away.

This story was previously published in the *Miami Herald.*

Photo by Tim Daw

The Lords of Dog Town

BRENDA WILSON

If you have not loved an animal, a part of your soul remains asleep.
—Proverb found on a signpost in Yelapa, Mexico

In the heart of the jungle and along the seashore, on the Bay of Banderas, the dogs of Yelapa tell a different story than your average, mangy, starving Mexican dog.

A few years ago, author Michael Pollan theorized in his book, *The Botany of Desire,* that seemingly-unconscious plants enlist the hearts and minds of humans to further their own agenda to thrive and multiply. Pollan cites examples of tulips that seduce us with their beauty, apples that endear us with their sweetness, and marijuana that intoxicates us with its heady compounds. I was reminded of this theory as I witnessed a similar, suspicious scenario playing out on *la playa de Yelapa* between the enormous stray dog population, the locals, and the affection-starved tourists.

I picked up the scent when I noticed that all the typical arch-enemies of dogs were vanquished and abolished. In Yelapa, there are no cars, no cats, no squirrels, no kennels, no leashes, or collars. There are no masters, no silly names, no license tags, no territories, no aggression, no dog catchers, no starvation, no diseases, no fences, no doghouses, no tethers. There are *no problemas!*

As I became aware of this canine *cosa nostra* phenomenon hidden in plain sight, I marveled at the stellar health of the *Canidae*. All the woofs were well fed with shiny coats, white teeth, and bright eyes—suggesting that they get plenty of guacamole, fresh fish, and pie! There is even a town vet who offers free services to the strays, deworming and neutering them twice a month. Wait, that is more healthcare than Americans receive!

The locals rise in the early mornings to wash the sidewalks clean of all the doggy and donkey debris that accumulated the day before. The dog-spotting *touristas y locales* provide hand-fed sustenance, while the pups crouch and pray to the local patron saint: Our Lady of Doggy Bags.

These Good Boys share a variety of duties around the tiny Mexican hamlet. After an initiation and a vow of silence, they are assigned a beat. They became the greeters, grounds-keepers, escorts, guides, clean-up crew, beach companions, fish dogs, cantina entertainment, plate patrol, port authorities, and bar bouncers. Some are even guides!

Case in point: I once got turned around in one of the Yelapa byways, trying to find the Yacht Club. A sleek German Shepard mix was napping on dried palm leaves at her post at the intersection where I stood perplexed. She opened one eye, rose from her nap, and began walking down the path. I followed and was then guided to the Yacht Club by the shepherdess. I am still unsure how she knew where I needed to go or how I found the trust to follow her. But the fact is, I was lost and she led me all the way to the hostess station. Perhaps most tourists get lost and she was merely performing a habitual task of guidance and kindness. Nonetheless, I gave my guide some pats of gratitude, and she smiled, wagged, and returned to her post in the crossway.

Since the dogs do not have official homes, they snuggle up under the *cerveza* tables on the sandy beach, or on the knoll to bask in the warm sunlight. The look in their eyes in the dawn light says: *would love to cuddle with you!*

On my last night, I dined at the BBQ joint where the dogs were working the scene, methodically sitting under every table to collect scraps and pats. This was a preferred eatery, and there were plenty of doggy bags on hustle. It was obvious that the dogs working the joint preferred to skip the doggy bag routine altogether and go straight for the hand-feed under the table. *Mi amor,* Tim, and I made friends with the silky, buff, male terrier with a blonde mustache and underbite sitting under our table. The Wiley Woof was suave and even perhaps psychic. Noticing his polite and attentive demeanor, Tim joked "at least he is not begging." On cue, El Suave sat on his hound hind, paws up, begging, and posing for a picture with a deadpan stare. Cheeky.

Later, at the nearby bar, I noticed a small black fluffle-weiner with a tough attitude and a golden snaggle-tooth. He was The Heavy, packin' heat, running at a fast clip to nip the heels of an unruly patron. He escorted the wiseguy to the door. The success of the bounce sent El Doggo into a happy tailspin as he rejoined the fiesta in full wag. He accepted many a belly rub on the dance floor before dashing away to the kitchen and out of sight. I believe him to be perhaps Don Yelapa, the Hefe, or El Capo.

There is a rumor that even "kept" pooches elect to stray and go on the lam. Because what dog doesn't like to roam and comb the beaches and cantinas in search of friends and Scooby-snacks? The *Yelaperros* seem elevated in status—perhaps even part-human and probably part-angel. They are self-possessed, un-mastered, and self-mastered. By all appearances, they have achieved enlightenment and doggy-nirvana. They roam free without tether or strangle. They do not bark, snarl, growl, or struggle. They are fed and pet by many hands. These Doggy Boys have remastered the "man's best friend" idea and flipped it to make their bones. Akin to Pollan's musings about the wiley ways of our botanical friends, the *Canidae* have become road-kings instead of road-kill. Indeed, in Yelapa, the old saying holds true: *All Dogs go to Heaven.*

This essay appeared on the *Deep Travelogue* blog.

Photo by Tim Daw

Yelapa: where the sea & river meet
Photo by Lisa Boice

Between Yelapas

LISA BOICE

Bad luck came crashing down on me the moment I uttered the words to Christina.

"I meant it," Christina said. "You really should write a book about you and Steve and all your birding adventures!"

I answered a modest, "Thank you" for her compliment and then finally said out loud why I didn't think I could do it: "You know how every story needs a crisis?" I asked. "We don't have a crisis. We don't have that deep ravine in the story arc—where the narrative takes a nose dive because something horrible happens. You know, like divorce, or heaven forbid, cancer."

Those were the words I should not have said.

We were walking on the sandy shore in Yelapa, Mexico and we had just wrapped up a morning session of writing. We were part of a small group of women who were here to write, and we spent the first morning of our workshop taking turns reading what we had wildly scribbled in our notebooks. We were making our way back to our *casita*—one of a series of open-air dwellings at a place called Garcias Rentals—and I was going to meet up with my husband, Steve. He had spent his morning looking at all the birds through his binoculars from the hammock in our *casita*.

Most of what I had been writing was about Steve and

birding. My words were random vignettes about how he pulled me into his world of traveling in search of birds. I didn't know how to weave it all together in a book.

"What does one learn from a bunch of birding stories and adventures without a crisis?" I continued. "I don't want to wish for any of that."

"No," she assured me. "No you don't. But I don't think you need that."

"I don't know," I sighed. "I can't think of how it would work."

Someone else from our writing group caught up with us. I slowed down my pace and let the two walk ahead of me.

Yelapa is a small beach town in the southern cove of Bahia de Banderas—the same bay where you'll find Puerto Vallarta. You get to Yelapa by taking a 40-minute water taxi from Puerto Vallarta. In Yelapa there are no cars and no ATMs, and you find yourself accidentally calling it an island from time to time because the remoteness makes it feel like one. The locals are quick to correct you: "No, not an island," they say with an eye roll.

Most of Yelapa's visitors are tourists from Puerto Vallarta who come only for the day. They arrive crammed on excursion boats that drop them off on the beach directly in front of rows and rows of plastic beach loungers. The tourists spend their day listening to the thumping club music as they tan in the sun and order drinks. Locals zig-zag their way in between the beach loungers, peddling cases of jewelry, sarongs, and most famously, homemade slices of pie in big Tupperware containers.

The day visitors are found at one end of Yelapa's bay while our casitas were at the other end, where Steve and I could birdwatch from our living room.

Magnificent Frigatebirds were Yelapa's early risers, soaring above the sky each morning. They are the pirates of the bird world because they steal from other birds who did the work of hunting for food. Terns and gulls who were doing the job of diving for fish were easy targets for the frigatebirds who would yank on or nip at their tails and then swoop underneath to grab fish that fell from their victim's beaks. Black Vultures, however, took their time in the morning. They hung out in groups on the sand, fanning out their wings to dry the morning dew from their feathers and then spent the rest of their day circling above in search of thermals.

Then there was the lone Snowy Egret, always hunting for fish in the surf. Each time he lifted his feet out of the water, I would get excited to see his golden slippers. By the estuary, I could find at least 20 or so Yellow-Crowned Night Herons. A boat was anchored onto the sand, and on it a gang of six reliably appeared each day, shoulders hunched over like old men.

Each night I would fall asleep, satisfied with having the interesting problem of not having a crisis—of being happy and knowing that it was, perhaps, the best possible place to be.

◆◆◆

A year later, we arrived again to Yelapa. The water taxi had dropped us off at the shore where I was instructed to fling my right leg over the side of the boat at the bow and then, when the water receded, throw over my left leg. By some sort of miracle I did not fall when I did this, and I walked ashore through the surf directly toward Garcias. On the beach, I looked behind me and was relieved to see that Steve had made it off the boat OK. He was thinner than he was last year and more weak.

Six months earlier, between visits to Yelapa, Steve was diagnosed with prostate cancer. This is heavy news for anyone. But when examining the cancer through a CT scan, the doctors found another cancer—a different, completely unrelated one—growing on one of his kidneys. This was a faster, more aggressive cancer we were told, and the doctor would say, "You are so blessed that we found this when we did."

Steve had the first surgery to have the kidney cancer removed, and we were happy to hear that it hadn't spread further into his kidney. Two months later, Steve had his next surgery to have his prostate removed.

Once cancer walks through the door of your life, it lays down a heavy burden. While we were assured that it was all gone, our lives turned to looking over our shoulders, wondering when it was going to sneak back in. We felt vulnerable and stalked. *How do the birds manage life? I wondered. Do they look over their shoulder, knowing that at any moment their life could end in the jaws of a predator? How do they sing when they know their life can be cut short at any moment?*

During the months between the two Yelapa trips, I watched Steve's muscle slip away. The aftermath of the surgeries, the depletion of testosterone, and the loss of energy were preying on him. I could see the fear in his eyes, and conversations began more than once with, "When I die...."

"No one's dying right now," I'd snap back. "They got the cancers and you're clean."

"For now," he'd say.

That's the mental burden that accompanies the physical toll of cancer, and it had moved in as a permanent resident in our lives. I was compelled go back to Yelapa, though I wasn't sure why. Perhaps to somehow erase what I had said before.

◆ ◆ ◆

We stayed in the same room at Garcias we had stayed in before, and it felt like home: the same striped Mexican blankets, yellow walls, and Mexican tiles. The same round wooden dining table and chairs. The same hammock. And the same birds.

The same Snowy Egret I came to know last year walked the surf slowly, looking for his dinner. The swell crescendoed to a roar, then broke into a crash, leaving only a whisper of foam as the water slipped back into the bay and the egret scurried through the white blanket of bubbles looking for tiny fish. Over in the estuary, a trio of White Ibis slowly walked through the shallow water, poking their long beaks in the water looking like old ladies walking with canes.

A Reddish Egret fanned its wings over its head, using a technique referred to as canopy feeding. It danced like a maniac, running left then right then left again to stir up the fish.

Pie ladies still roamed the beaches selling pie out of big plastic bowls while locals peddled silver jewelry, rope hammocks and beautiful sarongs. Tourists came over for the day and filled up the rows of white plastic loungers at the touristy section of the beach.

But the beach had changed. The estuary flowed into the ocean, and during high tide it was impossible to cross on the beach. With sandals in one hand and grasping Steve's hand with my other hand, we walked through the estuary, right next to the ibis and egrets who paid no attention to us.

We walked by the Reddish Egret who was not spooked by our presence. A Night Heron hunted along the end of the estuary while frigatebirds pestered the terns and then soared above us and drew circles in the sky.

We reached the sandy edge of the water. We had to step up to the edge, and Steve grabbed my hand to help me on to the sand. I heard a song bird singing, and Steve looked over his shoulder automatically in the direction of the song.

"Mangrove Warbler," he said matter-of-factly.

He pulled his binoculars up to his eyes to locate the warbler. The warbler's song was familiar to me, and I closed my eyes to hear the song's mnemonic, "*Sweet, sweet, sweet. Life's so sweet.*" I could feel it beginning to erase those words I first uttered on the beach in Yelapa.

We started to walk away when the warbler stopped singing. Steve took my hand and we took a few steps, and the warbler began his recital again. We both looked back over our shoulders, but this time we weren't looking for cancer. We were looking for birds.

This essay appeared on the *Deep Travelogue* blog.

Magnificent Frigatebird
Photo by Lisa Boice

Alhambra interior, Granada
Photo by Omar Chennafi

PART THREE

Spain

Deep Travel Spain: In Search of Duende

What is *duende* and where do we find it? The great Spanish poet Federico García Lorca defined it as the dark beauty found in Andalusian art: the bullfight, the fierce flamenco dancing, and the strains of a guitar. You might recognize it closer to home in the haunting chords of your favorite Leonard Cohen song. Wherever we find it, *duende* can transform struggle into art and sorrow into revelation. For the past two years, Deep Travel has traveled to Lorca's hometown of Granada, Spain, and explored *duende* at its source. We visited the *gitano* caves, marveled at the Alhambra, and enjoyed a sunset paella party with local flamenco dancers in the Sacromonte. Our writing was infused with the *cante jondo*—the deep song at the heart of *duende*.

It Never Goes Quite Right

GLORIA WILSON

Gloria read this vignette during the first Deep Travel Spain workshop in a cave above Granada after a flamenco performance.

It never goes quite right. The wind shifts, the wave comes in, the ashes lie flat. The ever-present pressure of finding the perfect spot for deployment. The hill on the Serengeti or the elephant-demolished bush on the plain. High atop a cliff in Tibet or the holy hot spring. The bay that surrounds Robben Island or from Table Mountain. High or low, land or sea. Like the Buddhist air or water burials. No matter. The remains will eventually be swept away. I bring him in my pocket and release, to share the wondrous sights of places he would never know.

A friend is aghast! You've taken him everywhere? Tibet, India, South Africa, Peru, Chile, Ecuador, Argentina, France, Italy, Guatemala, Belize, Vietnam, Cambodia? Jerry will never be free if you don't dispose of all of his remains. I don't agree, but the admonition lingers.

My daughter and I talk of perfect places for the final burial. We nod. A not-so-far-away island off the coast of Massachusetts. Not exotic, but very familiar. An island getaway where the three of us often went, where we looked into the yachts at night, walked the cobblestone streets, imagined the wives waiting for the whalers coming home from sea. We will go again on Jerry's birthday to celebrate the lives we shared.

The high speed ferry takes but an hour. Exhilarated from the sea air and a bit anxious, we drop our bags at the bed and breakfast and go straight to the flower cart on the main street for some wild flowers. Next stop, our favorite sandwich shop.

With flowers, sandwiches, and beach towels we head to the beckoning light house. The one that greets the ferries and bids them goodbye. Perfect marker for the resting place. But it never goes quite right—we should have music, we should have written something to say. Once again we don't want to say goodbye.

In knee-deep water, I toss the ashes, Cait tosses the flowers. The wave comes in, the wind shifts, the ashes and flowers come back to us. We smile. It never goes quite right, but then it never goes quite wrong.

Taza Azul

STACY BOYINGTON

I am too tired to rush anything or to go anywhere on this grey, damp morning. Not even to *la cueva de Paco*, located just behind and up the path from my own cave dwelling. At Paco's, fresh juice lovingly squeezed from Granada oranges, hot black tea in an adorned silver pot, toast with butter, and sweet cake made by the invisible hands of Paco's sister await my arrival for breakfast. The round table in the dimly lit room where we dine and clumsily attempt to communicate between Spanish and English, is draped with a floor-length cloth, concealing an electric heater to warm our legs. This is one of many thoughtful gestures our morning host bestows upon us during these bone-chilling, rainy days of spring.

Though I slept as if in a coma, I wake in the windowless dark to fuzzy thoughts. Was it the *Rioja*, the late-night, meat-laden meal, the ten miles of walking up and down and up the hills again through cobblestone *calles?* Or is it a fatigue I carry with me across the oceans?

Emerging from my whitewashed gypsy cave, I scan the valley and I am astounded yet again by the magnificent umber palace which lies before me across the river. The Alhambra! This destination has called to me, tugged at my longing for a decade. Standing before its Moorish grandeur, I quietly acknowledge my providential presence.

I deeply breathe in the chilled air, blessing the day ahead and all the mystery it holds.

Turning away from the iron-gated entrance to my cave and the incessant crowing from the arrogant rooster perched upon it like a masthead on a ship, my blistered feet propel me down a single-file, earthen path. Thick blooms of spring mustard engulf me until I pass the neighborhood's once communal stone oven, and I reach the *carmens* of the Albaicín nestled below. I no longer need to think my way to Plaza Larga. My body holds the directional memory. The Albaicín wakes slowly. My gait matches its tempo.

Approaching the Plaza, I stop to buy miniature Spanish *palmieres* from the tiny *panaderia* and bright tangerines from the *mercado* across the street. These are the offerings I bring to share with "the real writers," the published masters who write novels, books of truth, articles for magazines, enchanted poems, online tales, and stories to entice travelers. They attend the workshop convening in the apartment above the inlaid pomegranate square, where I join them for our morning session. I write for no one.

Before settling in my chosen chair, I find the electric kettle in the kitchen and pour myself a cup of steaming water. I wrap my trembling hands around the heated mug to warm and calm my spinning thoughts.

On this morning, our facilitator, Erin, begins our workshop by asking us to close our eyes. She guides us to feel our hearts, to feel the *duende* which we have come in search of from far and wide. She persuades us to imagine our tender hearts immersed in warm water, then in water which reaches the boiling point, until all the water evaporates and we feel our hearts left in a scalding pan, scorched by flames. Horrified, I watch my heart turn from soft pink to rubber grey, to charred black. Yet, under the veil of char, a ventricle of crimson remains.

I want to stop! I want to rescue my seared, still-glowing heart before it is too late!

I open my eyes, relieved to return to the present where hope still exists.

My gaze settles on the warm cup I grasp, and I realize it is in fact a blue mug.

Prior to my departure from the San Francisco Bay, my treasured Oregonian friend, sensing my trepidation to actually participate in the writing during my upcoming adventures, said to me, "if all you write is 'blue mug,' it is enough. This is your journey. Find your way. You are enough."

Granada is forever my Blue Mug.

This story appeared on the *Deep Travelogue* blog.

The Alhambra at night
Photo by Omar Chennafi

Tinto de Verano

LAVINIA SPALDING

On a stark white balcony
in the Costa Del Sol
your wide-eyes averted mother
served us paella, heaping bowls
of seafood and saffron sun
with goblets of red wine
and lemon Fanta.
Tinto de Verano, you told me.
Wine of Summer.
I wanted to drink it
from your fingernails
the summer we pretended
we were not more
than teacher and student.
Pretended I had never
licked the bottoms of your feet
as we lay in tepid water
in the dark, the candles long before
drowned in waxen pools.
Pretended I'd never
wound my tongue methodically
around the ends of your hair,
wound my life

around the ends of your sentences.
Or slid my hands up your thin ankles
As you danced the *Sevillana* over me in bed,
your hips writing poetry in cursive,
your sinuous wrists reaching up
for an imaginary apple, plucking it
from an invisible tree, dropping it into
an illusory basket.
Just pretend, you said, and it's easy.
So we pretended it all
but happiness, but love,
and I spun around as you taught me,
but the music skipped
and I opened my eyes to find I was alone,
reaching for what was not there.

This poem was previously published in *Inkwell Journal.*

Flamenco performance during a Deep Travel party
in the caves above Granada
Photo by Anna Elkins

¡Olé!

MJ PRAMIK

"*Gólpe! Gólpe!*" demanded Virginia. "Shoulders back. Where is your head? *Marcando!*"

I began taking flamenco lessons as an experiment prior to my first trip to Spain. It was a *Why not?* endeavor, my trial-by-fire defiance of genetics, an attempt to transform my curvy Polish body and sensible personality into that of a vibrant and charismatic *bailaora*. I'd read that it takes three weeks of practice to effect a change in habit. Prior to my stay in Seville, my ultimate goal: to find the perfectly fitted shoes and svelte flamenco-*Semana–Santa–Feria* dress, thus achieving a massive metamorphosis. Why not dare to buck the odds?

Finding my San Francisco Bay Area class on the first day of my enrollment really tested my determination to study flamenco. Lines Dance Studio, host of Virginia Iglesias's Flamenco Academy of Dance, had moved from the location I'd visited to retrieve my ballerina daughter two decades before. It was no longer situated comfortably in the heart of the "safe" Civic Center neighborhood of San Francisco. This I didn't know. I drove around the central plaza several times and finally called.

"Oh, we moved years ago. We're on 7th Street, between Market and Mission," a velvety male voice crooned.

Zigzagging across Market Street, I realized the new location was in a building on the old skid row—one of the last blocks in San Francisco left untouched by the throngs of recent well-heeled transplants, likely due to the busy Social Security Administration building down the block and the sizeable heroin treatment center around the corner. Saturday at noon the street people slept in, and I wove through them as I hurried from my parked car to the sanctuary of an ancient brick building. The stair access was on lockdown; the only way up was an ancient elevator manned by a heavily tattooed millennial listening to tunes wafting from a crackly battery-powered radio.

Master teacher Virginia Iglesias possesses the patience of Job. For the past thirty years she has lived life rooted in her Spanish heritage, dedicating herself solely to the art of flamenco. Her website touts her extensive training at the most renowned flamenco academies in Madrid, where she began her professional dance career. She's choreographed for and performed with Spanish dance companies and toured internationally. Even today, she lives in Spain part of the year, a wise professorial choice for this wholly Spanish art form, I thought.

A gorgeous redhead of a mysteriously becoming age, Virginia held her head high and straight. Her posture oozed "professional dancer." Her bold printed skirt and turquoise flamenco shoes underscored her prowess. In the cavernous studio with long windows abutting the soaring ceiling, she was accompanied by Jorge Liceaga, musical director, *cantaor* and guitarist. Jorge hailed from Mexico City, and, like Virginia, has performed internationally for decades.

"Look in that closet; take this." Virginia handed me the key and pointed me toward a petite Alice-in-Wonderland wooden door in a pale green wall. Once unlocked, assorted flamenco shoes tumbled out. I scrounged for a matching pair, two well-worn, pinching Capezios. They'd do for my first lessons. I was taken aback by the tiny nails studding the toes and heels. So that's how they made all that noise!

Flamenco calls for strong hamstrings and elegant arms, neither of which I possess. Facing the front mirror, I stood in stark contrast with the poised style of my classmates, all women save one middle-aged man. They clearly knew the routine; I imitated to the best of my modest abilities.

"The more you practice, the stronger your hamstrings become," Virginia promised. "*Planta, planta.*"

"*Planta*-ing" one's foot is achieved by striking the ball onto the floor. A twinge of pain developed after only a few minutes. Slinking to the back of the room, I followed those before me. We repeated and reviewed each choreographic set. Jorge strummed the Spanish guitar as we students stomped across the worn wooden second floor of the 107-year-old building.

"*Palmas, palmas.*"

Hands clapped *sordas*—muffled pops made by cupped hands—or *secas*—strong, dry strikes. In theory, the *palmas* are syncopated with the rhythms of the music and the feet. But I've never been able to walk, pat my head, and rub my belly at the same time, so for each hour-long class I felt like a klutz.

"Focus only on the feet—just the feet. You can add the hands and arms later." Virginia peered straight ahead into the floor-length mirror and met my eyes from where I hid in the back row.

After the first class, and each one thereafter, I applied ice to my knees, then popped two ibuprofen. My knee brace did not add grace to my form. With steely determination, I arrived on time for every single lesson prior to my departure for Seville. *Ouch!* I did accomplish an authentic finger motion, which Virginia complimented, but the heel-drop *tacón* escaped me.

Flamenco has its roots in the music of the Romani people

who lived in the Punjab region of Northeast India, migrating westward circa 1000 BCE. Flamenco's rapid-fire foot movements are reminiscent of the stomping ankle-belled Indian *Kathak* dance form. Indian emigrations spread west over several hundreds of years, bleeding into the Balkans, Germany and France. Upon their arrival in northeastern Spain (near Barcelona) around the 15th century, these clans met with tribes who migrated out of Egypt, crossed the Straits of Gibraltar, and settled in Andalusia. These southern wanderers became known as *gitanos*—from the Spanish *egiptanos* or Egyptians—today's gypsies. Often persecuted and forced to move, these vagabonds were suspect to townspeople. Their plaintive song, *gitano*, decried their misery and misfortune. Usually sung by a single male, *gitano* comes out rough and raw. Only later, in the nineteenth century, did they don their boots and reaffirm this injustice in their fierce, hammering dance. Castanets entered the flamenco lexicon in the 1900s, as a tourist attraction.

Triana, the middle-class neighborhood across the Guadalquivir River from the posh tourist center of Seville, housed the gypsy tribes for centuries. In her excellent book, *A Cultural Journey Through Andalusia: From Granada to Seville*, Gwynne Edwards documents in detail the fascinating evolution of flamenco. My own initial experience with this history arrived when I wandered through Triana alone in the evening on my third night in Seville and heard a *siguirya (cante grande)*, the saddest and darkest of gypsy songs, wafting from the window of a café. The intensity and heartbreaking tone reminded me of the *siguirya* described by Edwards:

- *Cuando yo me muera:* When I come to die
- *te pío un encargo:* I ask of you one favor
- *que con las trenzas de tu pelo negro:* that with the braids of your black hair

- *me marren las manos:* they tie my hands.

A visit to the Museum of Flamenco Dance welcomed me into the world of flamenco in a different way than my feeble attempts at *gólpe* and *palmas* did. Historical presentations of the flamenco greats, frayed costumes rescued from several hundred years of dance, and videos of the specific strains of technique further opened this realm to me. That evening I watched four performers of classical flamenco at Casa Del Flamenco in the Barrio de Santa Cruz, also known as the *juderia*, the former Jewish Quarter. On the stage, a large, square, raised-wooden structure, four colorful chairs for the dancers sat across from the audience, who were seated around three sides. The Andalusian tiles adorning the walls provided a richly textured background for the beautiful *bailaora*, in white blouse and a polka-dotted flounce skirt like those I'd already seen in many shops. Her three male counterparts dressed in black. Her tall handsome partner in the *Sevillanas*—the light and lively social dancing enjoyed at Seville's April *Feria* and weddings—added a black jacket.

I decided to return for a second performance two evenings later, which proved more intense and captivating. All performers, mostly attired in black, channeled the gypsy angst and isolation. The male singer in particular gave voice to their ancestral pain as his high-pitched yet deep-throated wail plunged those seated around him into the anguish of their existence. The last *cante chico* dance between a woman and young man did allow some joy, *allegria*, to creep back onto the dark stage. Their footwork blazed across the polished floor.

Wandering home that night from the nearby Catedral de Santa María de la Sede and window-shopping in the dark, I spied the perfect flamenco dress. *My colors.* I'd always known the classic red-and-black polka-dotted standards didn't fit my personality, but I didn't know what I was seeking until that moment. This *Feria* dress oozed sexiness in apricot, turquoise and deep blue. In that shop window, even the headless mannequin wore it well. This was *my* dress. Next to the mannequin hung a floor-to-ceiling photograph of a fetching, dark-haired young woman in profile, her hoop earring large and luscious. The shop name: Lina.

After returning to Hotel Casa Imperial, I traced the shop via smartphone with the aid of my techie roommate, Tania: Calle Lineros, numero 17.

I'm GPS-challenged, and Seville is far from a grid with a readable map. I had to ask for Calle Linares every five minutes, but I eventually rediscovered Lina on my own. The dress, in all its glory, still graced the front window. It being the week before *Semana Santa*, the shopkeepers calmly helped a steady stream of customers. After a short wait, I was able to beckon over a young woman and ask the price of the dress. Replying in Spanish, she showed me the tag. *Half of my April rent. Of course.* In addition, the hand-sewn mélange of colors and ruffles was meant for a much slimmer, taller woman. I reasoned with myself to do the sensible thing and walk straight out of the store. But before I left, I decided I needed to try it on…just once.

As I stood in front of the mirror hardly breathing, my mother's dictum crept into my mind: *You can't make a silk purse out of a sow's ear.* What my mother didn't know was that this feat of farfetched ambition had actually been accomplished in 1921. A team of creative scientists from MIT conducted an experiment to create "silk" from pork byproducts. Sevillanos, and all Spaniards, should appreciate this bizarre triumph, overloaded as their diet is with every form of pork imaginable—ham, prosciutto, bacon, and assorted "luncheon meats."

The MIT researchers had simply decided to do something everyone said was impossible, much like my decision to become a flamenco dancer, slither into a slimming dress, and shout ¡olé! The laboratory masters reduced over one hundred pounds of sows' ears—I kid you not; their raw material garnered a certification from Wilson and Co., a Chicago meatpacker who supplied the ears—to ten pounds of glue. Trial and error led them to devising a means to create strands of "silk" from the glue by imitating the silkworms' process. They spun these strands into cloth from which two silk purses were created in medieval designs. These wildly motivated academics hadn't given up. Neither would I.

"I'll take the dress."

The blond salesperson, in elegant pantsuit and patterned silk scarf, read me the price again to make sure I'd heard her correctly.

"Sí, sí." I stood in a trance.

The seamstress was summoned. Rocío Montero descended the stairs with a regal carriage; she was the older sister of the elegant blonde, Mila. I liked her immediately. She spoke little English, and I spoke less Spanish. She wore sensible working-woman shoes and the requisite colorful scarf. And glasses. Like I do.

"No worry, no worry. We fix it. Will fit." She smiled, quickly ripped out the stitches in all seams and began to pin and pin. In less than ten minutes she'd collected all my dimensions, the same kind of red tomato pincushion my mother had worn for years wrapped around her left wrist.

The sisters nodded together, smiling at me as I drooped in the bedraggled layers of crinoline. The voluminous garment weighed down my shoulders. As I stood there, wilting, beginning to waver in my commitment, I noticed a photograph on the back of the atelier: a wall-length black and white portrait of Princess Grace of Monaco descending a staircase on the arm of Prince Rainier. Smiling broadly, she wore a white Feria dress, all ruffles and eyeleted lace. I caught Rocío's eye and gestured to the picture.

"Sí, our mother made the dress for her."

I was certainly in capable hands.

Two days later I hurried back to Lina at seven o'clock after a long day of travels outside the city. The sisters had stayed open late for me. Much to my shock, the dress did not fit—too low cut up front, too long, too baggy.

I was heartbroken, but Rocío smiled reassuringly. "No worry, no worry."

She pinned and tucked yet again. I would leave Seville in a day and a half, no time for another fitting. We negotiated that they would ship the dress to San Francisco, keeping our fingers crossed. As a parting gift, Rocío presented me with a pair of red crystal earrings surrounded by stones the color of the ruffles on my dress.

The dress appeared at the front door of my San Francisco flat eight days later. The magnificent turquoise-coral-green-deep-blue silk flounces and circular cuffs were nestled in a large box of tulle-like tissue. I held my breath in anticipation…and of course, it fit perfectly. I sighed with relief and a deep sense of fulfillment. Who said I couldn't become a silk purse?

Now back to the hard work of the *gólpe* and *palmas*. My next session at Virginia's will test my stamina and grit, as always. But I now step into each flamenco lesson more hopeful that I can transform myself into an expressive, vivacious dancer. I have a dress to live up to.

This story was previously published in the anthology *Wandering in Andalusia: The Soul of Southern Spain* (Wanderland Writers, 2016).

Convivencia

CHRISTINA AMMON

Last spring I followed my friend Anna to the town of Ávila, Spain where she'd felt called to research the 15th-century mystic Saint Teresa. Anna had read Saint Teresa's seminal work, *The Interior Castle*, in her twenties and was captured by the nun's blueprint of the soul as a many-roomed castle, the center of which could be entered through the gateways of prayer and meditation. By going straight to the source—to the very convent where the Carmelite nun lived, to the cobbled lanes she'd walked, to the cathedrals where she'd prayed, Anna hoped to find inspiration for a collection of poetry she aimed to write. "I also hope to get an epiphany myself," she admitted.

I held no personal ambitions for the trip, but loved the concept of traveling to a place for artistic inspiration—even as a tagalong. So although this "town of stones and saints" wasn't my personal pilgrimage, when we arrived to the picturesque city on a sunny spring afternoon, I was happy to be there. We'd just finished up leading a group of twelve travelers through Morocco, and so quiet, unstructured time in a tranquil city seemed like the perfect way to unwind. Tapas bars lined the old streets, wide squares were clustered with silver chairs and conversation, and there was that warm honey light that felt so quintessentially Spain.

We trundled our suitcases from the train station until the pavement of the new city yielded to cobblestone inside the old, walled part of town. Our apartment was in Santa Teresa Square, and we were relieved on arrival to find a spacious living room with a wide window. Best of all, there were two separate bedrooms.

To cut costs, Anna and I mostly share rooms when we travel, an arrangement which works surprisingly well given that we are opposites in many—if not most—ways. For example, Anna cleans while she cooks, while I prefer to do the dishes after. She hangs her clothes in the closet straight away, while I work straight from my suitcase. And when the trash is almost full, she takes it out, while I wait till it is overfull. In sum: I'm messy and Anna is neat. But these surface differences are easily resolved, and I rein in my mess the best I can.

The real secret to our harmony is in our quiet style of traveling. We spend whole days apart, solitary *flâneurs* who keep good company with journals until dinnertime. Then over glasses of *Rioja* and wedges of *manchego*, we unpack the day's ideas and adventures. Perhaps most important, though, was that we share the same killjoy early-to-bed and early-to-rise circadian rhythm. Our idea of a great night is to nest in with a book.

Still, four weeks traveling together is a very long time, and since every traveler must pin her drifting existential discontent on something, a travel companion—even a perfect one—is an easy target. In fact, it was Anna's very perfection that I began to hone in on, imagining it was being imposed on me in the form of seemingly innocuous statements, which I took as cloaked suggestions. "I am going to go to the bathroom now—you never know, there might not be one on the bus!" she'd declare. Or she'd pour a can of nuts into a Ziplock saying, "It's always good to bring a snack on the train!"

I even found myself sighing at her perfect eating habits—the whole kernel oatmeal that she'd soak each night before going to bed. *Why not a carefree cinnamon bun, or a naughty, sugar-laced churro?* I wondered.

After taking stock of the apartment and enjoying the bright view of the square, we picked rooms and began to freshen up. In my own space now and free to be me, I stationed my overstuffed suitcase on the floor and let its contents eviscerate across the tiles. After my shower, I tossed a wet towel across my bed in gleeful rebellion.

Come afternoon, we wandered together out into the square, each with our respective books. Anna had Teresa's *Interior Castle,* of course, and I carried *The Dream at the End of the World*, a book by Michelle Green about Paul Bowles and the Lost Generation in Tangier, Morocco. It had been given to me by our travel group in Morocco and was the perfect gift. Since college, I'd been captured with Bowles and his rowdy and defiant literary comrades—Kerouac and Burroughs. Their rebellion echoed my own discontent with society, and the lawless zone that was Tangier in the fifties seemed an enchanting place to question mainstream norms. I'd cracked the book open back when we were in Fez the week before, continued it in Tangier, and now, nearing the end of the book, was eager to finish it.

We found a table in the square and ordered. Anna opened her heavily marked copy of *The Interior Castle*, and I resumed the section describing Woolworth heiress Barbara Hutton's elaborate *fêtes*. At her mansion above Tangier, Hutton dazzled guests like Truman Capote with belly dancers, camel drivers, nomadic tribesman, monkeys, and snake charmers. As usual, drugs, sex, and guns were in ample supply.

I looked up from my pages and chuckled at the opposite nature of our books. While in Anna's book the 15th-century Saint Teresa furnished her metaphoric interior castle with virtue and penance, the characters in my pages cavorted and indulged in actual brick-and-mortar castles. While Saint Teresa sought to make the monasteries stricter and more austere, in The City of Vice nothing was forbidden, except murder and rape.

After completing a chapter, I spooned my hot chocolate and wondered when I had last eaten fruit. "I think the last piece of fruit I had was in that dessert back in Tangier," I confessed, admiring Anna's porcelain complexion.

◆ ◆ ◆

The next day we split. I carried *The Dream at the End of the World* to a sidewalk café, and Anna set off to research Saint Teresa. I ordered an espresso and opened my book. Now Phyllis della Faille, a Tangier socialite, was chartering a cargo ship to ferry her menagerie of cats, rodents, horses and other pets to Portugal where she had just purchased an old castle. Like many of the Tangier expats living there in the '50s, Phyllis' life seemed so easy as to be borderline boring, and so she had to manufacture her own predicaments.

After a couple of chapters, I paid my bill and decided to take the audio tour of the impressive walls that earned Ávila UNESCO World Heritage status. I rented my headset at the tourist stand and ascended the stairs to begin my procession around the 2,516-meter long fortification. Along the way, I pushed numbered buttons and listened to historical commentaries through the earpiece.

Constructed between the 11th and 15th centuries to ward off Moorish invasions, the walls stood as a reminder of the religious conflicts between Morocco and Spain. The Moors took over the Iberian Peninsula in 711, and then the Christians took it back in the *Reconquista*. But there was a period starting in the 8th century, known as *La Convivencia* when everyone got along, and Muslims, Jews and Christians purportedly shared *Al-Andalus* in peace. This *Convivencia* broke down with the Inquisition, however, when even Saint Teresa herself was subject to interrogation. Her Jewish merchant grandfather made her suspect, as did her visions and spiritual ecstasies—which were seen as potentially false.

Church bells chimed, and I paused for a rest. I stared out at the Castilian plateau through the wall's crenellations, seeing vineyards, stone habitations and the Sierra Gredos Mountains in the distance. My thoughts returned to Paul Bowles and how much in my twenties I had admired his atheistic worldview. In his novel, *The Sheltering Sky,* his characters Kit and Port ventured into the vast Sahara to shed the fortifications of mainstream religion and ideologies and face down the Infinite straight-on. Bowles and his wife, Jane, did the very same thing in real life—smoking *kif,* taking *majoun* and courting the void among the dunes. It seemed so cool to me at the time—so honest and brave—and echoed my own youthful desire to shed my conservative religious Midwestern upbringing.

But a lot had happened to me in the intervening decades, and this was the first time I'd paused to take stock of my hero. Since then, I'd suffered broken-heartedness, periods of aimlessness, despair, and confusion about my purpose. A near-death paragliding accident left me with an increased sense of mortality, and with maturity, my political consciousness had evolved. I looked at the world with all of its violence and inequality and now wondered: *Why did evil exist and why was it allotted so unjustly?*

All at once, standing there on Ávila's walls, Bowles's vision of a world without meaning struck me as too harsh. In his world of no bounds, pleasures were pursued without limits, and Morocco was merely a decorative playground he and his friends could indulge cheaply and lawlessly. They bought mansions, collected expensive rare fish, and carried out their gin fizz lifestyles. Meanwhile, riots waged in the background as impoverished Moroccans struggled to wrest their independence from the French colonists.

Perhaps this deep lifestyle of denial is why, in *The Sheltering Sky*, Bowle's character Kit goes insane in the desert at the end of the book or why, in real life, Barbara Hutton attempted suicide twice. Maybe it's why Burroughs stayed high on opium all the time, or why so many of the expats that inspired Bowle's books were so disaffected. As a *Spectator* reviewer said of Bowles book, *Let it Come Down*, "As a morality about the mess people can get into who believe neither in this life or in any other, [it] has lots to say, but I do not see that much is gained by assembling a crowd of rootless creatures in a swamp and letting them rot." An acerbic commentary, for sure, but perhaps the reviewer was right: an undeniable undercurrent of despair ran through the Tangier scene.

♦ ♦ ♦

That night, Anna and I convened for dinner. We ordered a round of tapas, and she told me about her day—about visiting cathedrals and the convent where she viewed Saint Teresa's wooden pillow. She then announced that online check-in was available for our flight, and perhaps we should return to the apartment and log onto the Internet to avoid hassles at the airport the next day.

But before we turned in, we took one last stroll to admire Ávila's walls, now lit from the bottom in evening light. She loved Ávila and now felt inspired to write her book of poetry about Saint Teresa. I, too, felt inspired and confessed my unexpected revelation.

"I think I have outgrown nihilism," I declared.

♦ ♦ ♦

On the train to Madrid the next day, Anna pulled a tissue out and began wiping down the greasy window, reminding me again of how opposite we were. It never would have occurred to me to wipe down the window. But as the train lurched forward and we entered orchards hung with bright oranges, I was happy for the clearer view.

As the train coursed through the arid hills of Andalusia, I realized that we now had more in common. Though I wasn't going to adopt Saint Teresa as my new hero anytime soon, I could suddenly empathize with my friend's more ordered and meaningful view of the world.

What the meaning was I didn't know, but I suspected at the very least it involved kindness, the indispensible ingredient that seemed to elude the expats in Tangier. I pulled out a round of the *Casera* cheese I'd purchased in the square and Anna produced some crackers from her bag. And then we ate, drank, and in the spirit of *convivencia*, resumed our reading.

This story won a Gold Solas Award under the title "Fortifications."

The ramparts & walls of Ávila
Photo by Anna Elkins

The Poet & the Bloodstone

ANNA ELKINS

Saint Teresa of Ávila and Charles-Axel Guillaumot never met. She was a Spanish nun who lived from 1515-1582; he was a French architect who lived from 1730-1807. Each of them built and left a largely invisible legacy. Hers was a vision of the interior castle of the spirit within us. His was to save Paris from collapsing back into the quarries beneath it by building a support city belowground. Today, you can read what Teresa built with her words, and you can visit a fraction of Paris' abandoned quarries open to the public. In the poetry collection, Hope of Stones, *you are invited to enter a cross-century conversation among The Nun, The Architect, & The Poet. This poem is from that collection.*

Ávila, Spain

Today is research day. First, The Nun's museum.
It brims with depictions of heaven speaking
to the saint. In paintings, doves & rays of light
descend & suspend above her upturned face.
Speech ribbons unfurl toward her from angels.
The saint was known to levitate, so I half expect
the painted words to lift from their composition
& twirl about. They stay put.

      Next, the *Catedral
de Ávila.* Here, I see the grandeur The Nun left

behind. This church was built with bloodstone—
granite shot through with iron. It looks like
history has bled across the walls. The stone came
from a nearby quarry, & I think of The Architect.
What we pull from the earth & what we do with it.
I sit a long while on a hard pew, but my most
profound thought is how best to get to the train
station tomorrow.

                        Time to search for gazpacho
& *Rioja*—things that *don't* last for centuries. I keep
forgetting that in this country, I'm an outsider
trying to dine before nine.

                        The Nun founded
her simple convent outside the city walls.
Paris thought The Architect an outsider for not
being born in France. I am always looking
for what lies outside—even dining hours.

                                        I find
an open café & order wine the color of bloodstone.

Hope of Stones was a finalist for the Tupelo Press 2019 Dorset Prize.

Flamenco dancer in Granada
Photo by Omar Chennafi

Dancing with *Duende*

MIKE BERNHARDT

Esther Marin greeted me with a kiss on each cheek when she arrived at Restaurant Zoraya. We were in the heart of Granada's Albaicín—the labyrinthine, walled city built by the Moors who once controlled southern Spain. Catching up on news with our mutual friend, Esther's face broke into a huge grin as she lifted her sweater, showing off her barely-visible pregnancy. She was in her 30s with long dark hair, joyful eyes, and a strong nose. Esther was one of the preeminent flamenco dancers in Granada, along with her husband, Luis de Luis, and another dancer, Claudia Cruz. I was about to see them dance.

Before I visited Granada, I had only a vague, stereotypical idea of flamenco: a lot of posturing with long-stemmed roses, castanets, and loud stamping of shoes. But according to Spanish poet Federico García Lorca, truly authentic flamenco and its accompanying *cante jondo*—deep song—is full of *duende*.

Duende is a "mysterious power which everyone senses and no philosopher explains,"[1] Lorca said. "There are neither maps nor exercises to help us find the duende. We only know that he burns the blood like a poultice of broken glass."[2] *Duende* lives in the "tears of blood" that we cry when our hearts are broken. It's in the hush of the spectators when a bull looks defiantly at a matador in the moments before the sword is plunged into its heart. "The duende does not come at all unless he sees that death is possible,"[3] Lorca wrote.

For someone who was supposed to exude *duende*, Esther seemed surprisingly *happy*.

◆ ◆ ◆

Decades earlier my first wife, Susan, died unexpectedly when she was thirty-one years old. I felt utterly lost without the warmth in her eyes, her strength, and her wicked sense of humor. Writing poetry enabled me to express my grief, to survive the raging storms that engulfed me. As the storms subsided and I gradually built a new life, I sometimes missed the creative richness my pain had nourished. My poetry became barren without grief to fertilize it. Eventually I remarried, had a son, began a new career, and my writing slowed. Then it stopped completely.

Twenty-five years later I began to write again, this time prose inspired by various travel adventures. But sometimes, I wanted to convey deep emotional impressions and couldn't find the words. Something in me stirred while reading

---

[1] Lorca, Federico García. *In Search of Duende.* New Directions. 1998, p. 57. Lorca references Goethe's definition of *duende*.
[2] Lorca, p. 60.
[3] Lorca, p. 67.

Lorca's essays that I couldn't quite grasp, an intuition just beyond reach. I wondered if I had unknowingly accessed *duende* in my earlier writing, and if that was what I needed to find again. Spending a week in Granada with some writer friends, I hoped I might rediscover that mysterious power and use it to add more vibrancy to my work.

◆◆◆

We sat at tables at the back of the restaurant, facing a small stage. I was seated front and center, with just enough room between my feet and the proscenium for waiters to pass. A man and a woman, both dressed in black slacks and shirts and about the same age as Esther, sat down in chairs against the back wall of the stage. The man began to play his guitar.

Alternating between gentle and passionate strums, his music filled the room. It spoke of love, loss, and an excruciating sense of mortality: of lives lived in minor keys. His fingers burned with grieving arpeggios until after several minutes, he slowed. The woman began to sing—no, she wailed, screamed, and cried. I couldn't understand the words, but the emotion in her voice told me everything; I could feel her cries inside me.

Esther entered, dressed all in black except for her flowered shawl. Her face no longer held a smile; now it carried the weight of lifetimes of struggle. Her black shoes clacked on the floor as she stepped slowly at first, deliberately. She turned and held a pose, face turned up to the sky, brow furrowed, eyes closed. Some in the audience yelled "¡Olé!" Her face lowered again, she twirled her shawl around herself, then threw it back onto her shoulders. Her feet began to move, percussing complex patterns on the floor, increasing in speed until her calves and feet were a blur while her hands and fingers traced arcs above her head. Dance, guitar, and voice all combined into a soaring symphony of passion. A final pose, a slow graceful turn, a final *"¡Olé!"* from the audience.

Esther sat down, and Luis came out. Tall and slender with shoulder-length brown hair, he wore a fitted black jacket, an open-collared white shirt, and a buttoned pinstripe vest. A small patterned scarf was tied loosely around his neck. He gently clapped to the rhythm of the music, then began slowly stamping his heeled black boots. One hand was balled into a fist at his waist, the other was held out in front of him, fingers pointing down as they snapped to the rhythm. He threw his hands into the air, then down again, and stood for a moment with a haughty look as if to say, "You mean nothing to me!" The audience roared *"¡OLÉ!"*

His dance grew increasingly wild as he threw himself around in athletic twists, jumping twirls, and thigh slaps. I could feel that this wasn't rehearsed; he was dancing like the flames that seemed to burn inside him. All at once he leaped forward and hovered over the front of the stage, his face completely drenched in sweat and covered with his matted hair, teeth bared like a wolf about to lunge at me. It was so terrifying that I flinched. *"¡OLÉ!"*

He backed up, and in a moment of catching his breath, his eyes briefly flashed to Esther, who was sitting in the chair behind him. I saw the faintest of smiles cross her face and vanish. It wasn't until later that I would understand that exchange.

Now Claudia began to dance, her blonde hair framing a scowl accented with bright-red lipstick and a red dress. I thought she looked overdone—too much grimacing, too much makeup. Then she looked directly at me and smiled. But her eyes weren't smiling. They looked dangerous. Her eyes still holding mine, she snapped her dress across her legs with a loud *CRACK!*

Though she was eight feet away I felt an almost physical impact, as if she had conjured some dark force from within herself and flung it out at me. I was stunned and confused. She turned away and continued her dancing, but I could remember nothing from the rest of her performance.

That night, I couldn't sleep. I needed to write about what I'd experienced, and poetry came. I wrote a line and turned off the light. But over and over, the images demanded expression and the light turned on, off, on, off. It was 2:30 AM when I finally finished:

> She looked at me and smiled,
> the way fire smiles at dry kindling,
> fingers curling like the smoke of burning centuries.
> The vocalist wailed grief and joy to the black night
> as the guitar wrapped her in a compassionate embrace.
>
> She whipped her dress with a loud snap
> like a slack sail catching a sudden gust of wind,
> the deadly flap of a leathery dragon wing.
> I felt the force of it fly right through me,
> A demon screaming through the room.

Over the next few days, I tried to understand what had happened. How could Claudia have affected me so, the mere flap of her dress buffeting my soul? How could Esther transform herself the way she did, and what enabled Luis to improvise with such emotional intensity? I wondered if they had surrendered to some dark, creative presence inside themselves. Perhaps this was what *duende* meant.

I remembered a poem called "Sunday" that I'd written the year after my wife's death. For months after Susan died, I was occasionally blindsided by waves of shock so intense that I'd feel faint. One day I sat down, let the memories and feelings arise, and poured them onto paper. Like a shamanic spirit trap, the writing of it captured it all, and freed me. Though I continued to grieve, I never experienced that shock again.

I hadn't looked at "Sunday" in years, but that morning in

Granada, I knew: my *duende* was there. I decided to read the poem to my friend Tania. As soon as I spoke the first line, my eyes filled with tears. It was as if I were reaching into that spirit trap and finding everything I'd left there: the shock, the grief, the despair I'd felt the morning Susan died. It took me a long time to get through the poem; Tania was patient as words kept getting caught in my throat and I forced back sobs. I spent the rest of the day feeling cotton-headed and emotionally wrung out. And yet...I'd been seduced by my old muse and we had danced.

◆ ◆ ◆

In the hillsides above the Albaicín called San Miguel and Sacromonte, Romani people have lived for centuries in caves they often excavated themselves. In Granada, those I met were proud to call themselves *gitanos*. Long before Lorca brought flamenco and *cante jondo* to the world's attention, *gitanos* were dancing and singing in those caves, blending the grief of their difficult history with Arabic influences and the indigenous music of Andalusia.

On my final afternoon in Granada, our group visited one of the caves, a residence occupied by the same family for at least four generations. A dirt footpath switch-backed upward from the Albaicín's cobblestoned streets, through a waist-high meadow exploding with yellow mustard blooms, before passing the cave's wrought-iron gate. A lush terrace was partially shaded by arbors and covered with potted herbs and flowers, with a mesmerizing view over the Alhambra—that massive, ochre-walled, jewel of medieval Islamic architecture. A painted green door opened into a bright living room finished in white plaster and decorated with artwork and pottery.

Inside, a father and son sang and played guitar while a woman danced, passionately twirling and stamping on the stone-tiled floor. Her serious demeanor was softened by frequent smiles. She lit up the room. Neighbors gathered in the doorway to watch. The *gitano* owner of the cave stood up and the guitarist accompanied him as he sang a traditional song with all his might in a rough tenor voice, his hands on his heart, his face beaming as everyone cheered and yelled *"¡Olé!"* every time he finished a stanza. I was experiencing flamenco as it might have been long ago: a celebration of life performed not on a stage, but in a home with friends and community.

I realized that just as Esther's delight in being pregnant hadn't been a barrier to expressing her *duende,* I didn't have to spend every day shedding tears of blood to find my own. Maybe I could draw on my pain the way a painter fills his palette, use it like the rarest, richest of colors, and then let it go. The finest flamenco artists seem to do this. Night after night, they fight their *duende* "hand-to-hand[4]... on the very rim of the well,"[5] as Lorca described it, then walk away seemingly unscathed. Luis seemed to have teetered between inspiration and madness as he danced on the edge of the stage in Restaurant Zoraya. Yet he found a moment to glance at his wife and receive a furtive smile in return.

After the performers and neighbors left, the sun began to set and the world outside the cave fell into shadow. We lit candles and settled into our seats for the evening. One by one, we stood up to share our written interpretations of *duende.*

I faced a room full of expectant faces. My stomach fluttered as if I were about to fall off of a cliff. And then as I began to read, the words I had written so long ago seemed

---

[4] Lorca, p. 62.
[5] Lorca, p. 67.

almost to rise up and carry themselves into the audience.

♦ ♦ ♦

Sunday

Together, we survived the terrifying night
of CPR and defibrillation, too many tubes and wires and doctors,
my kisses on your forehead and your eyes kissing me back
until your EKG exploded again and they told me to leave.
I sat outside in the hallway talking softly with you.

In the morning, though your eyes seemed empty,
I dreamed of your recovery and went home to sleep
only to be greeted by a ringing phone and an urgent voice
and I was out again, stuck in traffic on the Bay Bridge,

praying, screaming at God to get me to you in time.
Hoping that curses and prayers might be enough,
I inched and fought my way through traffic and despair
until finally free, nearly drowning

I plunged into the streets racing
to San Francisco General. Sometimes now
I like to imagine what I would have told the police
if they'd noticed. I like to think that I wouldn't have pulled over

I would've just plummeted on at
70 miles per hour up Potrero Avenue letting
them catch up to me in the parking lot as
I ran inside MY WIFE'S DYING! I would've screamed

but they didn't notice.
I ran inside alone
to find my friends crying
and you, dead.

♦ ♦ ♦

In flamenco, *duende* might reveal itself in the terrifying snap of a dress. In writing, it might mean spending hours—or months—honing a single paragraph to the point where the words leap off the page, dripping sweat and baring their teeth like Luis. And it might be found in a cave, when a man shares his raw heart with his audience and they receive it with tenderness and respect.

When I was done reading, I looked around at my friends. I felt drained, relieved to have finished, and deeply alive. I glanced at Tania. Unlike Esther at Restaurant Zoraya, she made no effort to hide her smile.

This story won a Bronze Solas Award. The poem "Sunday" was published the anthology *Voices of the Grieving Heart* (Cypress Point Press, 1994) and *Finding What You Didn't Lose* (Tarcher/Putnam, 1995).

Luis de Luis dancing flamenco at Jardines de Zoraya in Granada
Photo by Mike Bernhardt

Rooftops of the medina through the crenellations of Riad Laayoun,
Fez, Morocco
Photo by Siobhann Bellinger

PART FOUR

Morocco

Deep Travel Morocco: The Art of Adventure

Each year, Deep Travel explores the art of adventure in sensory-rich Morocco. We begin our writing workshop in the Fez Medina—a UNESCO World Heritage Site of over 9,000 byways. From there, we venture into the Middle Atlas for some retreat time in the mountain village of Moulay Idriss. While in Moulay, we visit the 2,000-year-old Roman ruins of Volubilis, tour Morocco's wine country, and enjoy daily life in this small, enchanting city before returning to Fez. Along the way, we meet local artists, restaurateurs, change-makers, and traditional storytellers.

Because Circles Close

LAURA HUGHES

I spend my last day in Fez under the sun,
on a blue-tiled terrace,
across from a fortress,
up a hill of olive trees,
over medina rooftops,
drinking Cava, straight
from a small bottle, carried
over the sea—unchilled.

I wear the dress I wore
at the start—on a Spanish terrace,
surrounded by geraniums,
watching the sun set
beyond another fortress,
across other rooftops,
while a new friend swilled
from her own bottle.

Vignettes

DOT FISHER-SMITH

Dot Fisher-Smith has led Deep Travel Workshops in Morocco, Mexico, and Nepal. She can often be found with her journal on our trips, quietly recording her observations of our surroundings and the day's events. For some, a travel journal might form the basis for later writings. For Dot, journaling seems to be a way to get still and really "land" in a place. Either way, a journal makes an invaluable souvenir to enjoy back home. We love the freedom and artistry of Dot's entries, and we are happy that she was willing to share them here.

DAY (4) (1) 1:30 ON THE ROOF-TOP AGAIN
FROM EVERY WHERE
LOUD SPEAKERS BLARE
THE CALL TO PRAYER
IT FILLS THE AIR

I'VE TRAVELED ALL MY LIFE, IT SEEMS, TO FEEL,
ON THIS ROOF-TOP IN FES, THE FULLNESS
OF SATISFACTION I'M FEELING NOW
RIGHT HERE, IN MY BELLY, IN MY BONES
ON THIS BENCH, MY BUTT ON THESE CUSHIONS
MY CROSSED LEGS FUSED AT THE ANKLES
THIS SONG TO MYSELF — THIS BIRD AT MY FEET!

144

→ STANDING STILL

→ WATCHING BIRDS—

NO. THAT WAS LATER

FIRST, STANDING STILL AT

THE EDGE OF THE SURF, WATCHING—

STANDING STILL IN IT, I MEAN

STUDYING — WATCHING EACH WAVE

THE TIDE - IS IT COMING IN OR GOING OU

STANDING STILL, MAKING FRIENDS WITH

OLD FEARS, HOLDING MY PLACE

WHILE THE UNDERTOW SUCKS AT MY FEE

SINKING THEM IN THE SAND

NO RUNNING AWAY

BREATHING THROUGH

THE SURGING, UNDULATING

SWELLING SO WHOLE BACK

SHEET OF WATER

THEN CRASHING—

INTO BILLIONS OF
INTO FRAGMENTS
OF FOAM

SLOW WRITING

SLOW WALK
SLOWLY I

BEHIND THE BEACHFRONT
RESTAURANT'S

(THROUGH THE KITCHENS)

BETWEEN THE KITCHENS
LOS BAÑOS   EL CLIENTE
ONLY FOR EL CLIENTE

AND BEHIND THE KITCHENS ARE
WHERE THE COOKS AND SERVERS LIVE

THEIR FAMILIES, DOGS AND CHILDREN—

(SLOW WALK SLOWLY I ALONG THE PATH)

ALONG THE PATH
SANDY
THROUGH THE VILLAGE

WINDOWS, LOCKS, DOORS, GATES

EVERYWHERE THE SAME AND DIFFERENT

AN OYSTER SHELL,

AN EGG-SHELL

SIDE BY SIDE
IN THE SAND
AT THE EDGE
OF THE PATH

AS SHADOWS RISE ACROSS THE RIVER ON THE HILLS (SURF)

BIRDS PARTING TOGETHER ON THE SURFACE (SURF)

(GOING SLOW)

AS SHADOWS RISE ABOUT

5:15+ THE AFTERNOON   WATCHING WAVES STRUNG
A SECOND SESSION (BEING) PRESENCE
OO EXPERIENCE STILL—

EVERY O—O—O—O DAY OF PRACTICING (BEING) TOO   (YAK)
THE SUTRA ARE 2/3 UP THE HILLS AND OFTEN
THE SHADOWS ARE 2/3 UP. THE RE TWO-LEGGED OR TEN
NO WORDS ABOUT BIRDS. THEY HAVE TRIED TO WALK, WHICH OFTEN
THE UNDERWATER DIES THAT FOR BENDING TO WALK
THE BLACK—OR FOR WHITE UNDERNEATH
THE BEADY JOINT STUMBLING   (LIKE WEAKENED)
NOW CAN ONLY SEE THE SUN
(MANY) LOOKS LIKE DRUNKEN STUMBLING THE TBR OF THE MIDDLE HILL

& RECITES THE EXPERIENCE

MAYBE CAUGHT IN THE SPELL OF THE DESERT —
VAST EMPTINESS - OCHRE SAND - COBB STRUCTURES.
SPELL-BINDING SUNSET COMPLETE W/ CAMEL SILHOUETTES
PARADING SLOWLY ACROSS THE FLAMING ORANGE-RED STREAK OF
SKY, THEIR HERDERS CLOSE BEHIND — THEN WATCHING
THE AWFUL BEDDING-DOWN PROCESS...

. CAMELS ARE VERY STRANGE CREATURES — ESPECIALLY
AT DUSK.

NOW FOR BEDDING-ME DOWN ON MY TERRACE
UNDER THE HALF MOON & STARS. LOGISTICS FIRST.

5K ... DISTILLING THE DAY, SLOWLY DIMMING LIGHT. EACH LETTER A DARING-PROBE — A STEP INTO THE DARKNESS — A LEAP INTO THE UNKNOWN. I'M MOURNING THE LOSS OF MY FAVORITE FINE POINT PEN. HOW DID I LOSE IT? WHERE DID IT GO? O JOY O RAPTURE UNFORSEEN I FOUND MY MAGIC SLOW PEN FALLEN IN THE BLANKET WHEN I GOT UP. Ahhhhh! SUCH SIMPLE JOYS.

THE PUSH AND PULL
OF THE WAVES, SWELL, SUBSIDE
SURGE AND TUG

SLOW WALK UP THE WIDE SHALLOW RIVER BED POOLS MEANDERING THROUGH THE SAND MARKED WITH FOOTPRINTS OF ALL SIZES. BIRD TRACKS, ANIMAL TRACKS, MOTORCYCLE TRACKS, NO BICYCLES HERE. QUIET UP THERE—NO WAVE SOUND, SO PEACEFUL, QUIET.

I FOLLOW MY LUCK
I AM A HOST
I AM A CONNECTOR
I AM A CONDUIT

THIS
GROUP
MORE OCTOPUS
THAN JELLYFISH

BIRDS
FEEDING
IN THE
LAGOON

BLACK-NECKED STILT
TRI-COLORED HERON
COMMON EGRET
SNOWY EGRET
IBIS

* GOING SLOW — THE ANSWER TO EVERYTHING
  — THE REMEDY FOR ANXIETY
        THE FUNDAMENTAL DIS-EASE
                    (HUMAN)

                                            *

* DOT'S DICTUM!

149

Sister

KIMBERLEY LOVATO

Lahsan streams hot tea from an ornate silver pot into a colored glass stuffed with fresh mint leaves and sugar cubes, and sets it on the table.

"This is your last night in Maroc, Sister. What you think?" Lahsan asks in accented English, using the French word for Morocco and the name he's called me since we first met.

"I've fallen under the spell," I say. "I especially love your city of Fez and can't wait to return."

Lahsan's brows press together when hearing my slang and brisk speech so I simplify and speak slowly.

"I love it here," I say. "Thank you."

His eyes spark with comprehension and he places a blue and white plate of cookies in front of me, then puts his hand over his heart.

"You are most welcome back Sister," he says.

Dressed in a long, burgundy-hued tunic and leather slippers, he shuffles through a doorway and out of sight, leaving me alone with my sugary tea in the *riad's* tile-encrusted courtyard.

◆ ◆ ◆

Only a week earlier I'd been lounging on a metal chair in the Tuileries Gardens in Paris, when my phone rang. I recognized the number right away, and since I hadn't talked to my brother in months, I answered.

"Hey Rickley!"

"Hey Sis, how's it going? I hope I'm not bothering you, but I have a few questions about Paris."

"That's *so* weird," I said into the phone. "I'm actually *in* Paris right now."

He feigned surprise, but we both knew it wasn't really that weird. As twins, we were used to such uncanny coincidences.

A favorite movie of ours when we were growing up in the '70s was *Escape to Witch Mountain* in which twin brother and sister Tony and Tia move things without touching them and communicate with one another using only the power of their minds. As much as we wished we could speak telepathically during school or freak our mother out by rearranging the living room furniture from our bedrooms, it just wasn't our schtick. We once tried holding hands over our Formica kitchen table, silently imploring our cereal bowls to whirl like dervishes, but we couldn't provoke even a ripple in the milk.

In school, friends often asked me silly questions like, "Can you read your brother's mind?" or "If I punch you in the arm can he feel it?" I always said no, taking the questions at face value. It wasn't until I was much older, however, that I understood the curiosity behind these inquiries was the invisible link twins are perceived to have. It made sense. After all, we'd been together since the beginning, given a nine-month head start on forming a relationship while sharing a space the size of a watermelon, then set out on parallel paths through childhood and adolescence to endure the same stages and phases at the same time.

We not only share 50 percent of the same DNA and a

birthday, but until we were about two we also shared a room, our cribs pressed one against each wall, where my mother says we'd peer at each other through the slats. It was only when we hit double digits that our individual identities matured and the strings tethering us close lengthened, allowing us to drift in opposite directions. That's when the real understanding of our connection crystallized.

Mention walnuts today and the same disgusting image of him at about five or six years old vomiting into an ashtray pops into our minds. Put us in a pool together and we'll face each other and clasp hands, then jump to put our feet bottoms together. Our butts will eventually bump, and we'll summersault backward under water before surfacing, gasping for breath as we laugh. It's something we've done since we were kids, but neither of us remembers when or why it started. More recently, I'd locked myself out of the car after dinner with a friend. Instead of calling a taxi or a roadside service, which I'd normally do, I called my brother. He was working late and happened to be a few blocks from where I was stranded.

Now, here was my brother, a sound effects editor from California, calling me while I sat in a garden thousands of miles away in Paris to ask me what I knew about the subway stations in the French capital. I stood in the Paris Metro, holding my phone out while trains pushed and pulled air through the underground tube as they arrived and departed, letting the doors swish and thud open and close, then sent my brother the recording.

◆ ◆ ◆

Lahsan had started calling me Sister the morning after I arrived in Fez. I was chatting with Sue, the *riad's* manager, before setting out to explore the medina when Lahsan shouted from a balcony overlooking the courtyard.

"Sister, wait. I have something for you."

I nodded at him, then asked Sue if "Sister" was a perhaps a common term young men used to address female guests, or foreign women.

"Neither, and he doesn't say that to everyone," Sue said. "In fact I've never heard him call anyone that."

My heart warmed and fluttered, much like the lanterns that glimmered in the courtyard. I had been drawn to Lahsan immediately. Not in a romantic sense but in that way kindred spirits are when a connection is inexplicable yet undeniable. In everyday life back home, being called "Sister" by anyone other than my twin felt as threadbare as "yo, girlfriend!" or " what's up bro?" But when Lahsan said, "hi Sister," or "welcome back, Sister," which he did every time he saw me, I knew it came from a treasure chest deep inside him where his few English words were stored and selectively gifted.

"Sister, take this map," said Lahsan when he finally descended from upstairs to where I was standing with Sue. "If you get lost, I help you."

I unfolded it and began to laugh. It was a map of the medina, the walled-in old city of Fez, whose twisting narrow lanes took on the form and usefulness of cooked spaghetti noodles dropped onto a piece of paper.

"It's no problem," he said, interpreting my confused at my reaction.

In his long white tunic, Lahsan opened the front door and stepped into the sheltered lane that smelled of damp cement and forgotten daylight.

"You keep walking up," he said, pointing toward the invisible "there."

Outside, the medina walls were four and five stories high, and in some places the streets so narrow I could place my palms flat against the opposing cool stones. Beyond the *riad's* unmarked front door, I could see 25 feet ahead before the cobbled road cut right and disappeared. But getting lost in the medina's serpentine streets had been a "must" according to a friend who'd visited Fez before me. Not that I had much of a choice. I was disoriented within minutes and ditched the map soon after, imploring my curiosity to work as my compass.

When I'd first seen the medina from a distance, approaching from the outside in a taxi, it looked dehydrated; sun roasted to a golden hue the color of parchment paper; inert. But once through the keyhole gate and inside the thick walls, Fez came alive in a Pantone palette of colors, sounds, smells, and sights stitched together by the people who live and work in the cracks and crevices of a seemingly fathomless city. More than 9,000 streets, passageways, and dead-end lanes tangle and pucker through portals, and dive deep into souks where people squeeze through the narrows like toothpaste. At times, only the filtered fingers of sunlight through latticed ceilings reminded me there was sky above. Every inch was a turn of a living kaleidoscope whose sounds and colors reshaped in real time. An incessant clang and ting lured me to a tucked-away square one afternoon where metal craftsmen pummeled and plied at brass cauldrons from daylight to dusk. The arrhythmic beating vibrated the cavities in my teeth. Every now and then I'd poke my head into an open doorway to follow the tinkling of a fountain in a flower-filled courtyard. I sat in one garden where lemon and orange trees drooped with yellow and orange orbs, and let the citrus perfume waft up my nostrils. From windows above, floral curtains fluttered and children's clothes dangled on lines and whipped in the wind like prayer flags against the sapphire sky.

The song "Eye of the Tiger" rolled toward me down another unnamed street. For an instant, the music carried me back to the summer of 1982 and Niagara Street where by brother and I rode our bikes. We'd just seen the movie *Rocky*

III and as we pedaled up and down the sidewalk, we sang the lyrics and boxed at the air in tune with the song's opening instrumental salvos. The modern tune seemed incongruous in ancient Fez, but I eventually found the source of the music. It was literally a hole in a wall, as if a supersized Rocky Balboa himself had punched his giant fist through the stones. Inside, a boom box blared next to a 30-something-year-old man. A single swinging light bulb lit his nimble hands, which maneuvered a clacking wooden loom over colorful threads that would eventually transform into a scarf, or maybe a rug.

There were thousands of shops like this in the medina that, when shuttered, were almost indistinguishable from the stone from which they were hewn, and were easily absorbed into the human routine of disregard. Once opened, however, they bulged dirt to rafters with anything from sticky nougat candy, gold jewelry, ceramics, cooking utensils, spices and argan oil, to pointy leather *babouche* slippers in bubble gum colors. Bargaining was expected, but I was not good at it and paid way too many Moroccan dirhams, I was later told, for the *djellaba* I'd purchased.

"Sister, why didn't you tell me you were shopping, I would have gone with you," Lahsan said when I arrived back at the *riad*, a plastic bag in hand.

"It's OK. I don't mind going alone."

"No," said Lahsan, putting his hand on his heart. "It's my job to help you, Sister."

"*Shukran* (thank you)," I managed to say to him in Darija, Moroccan Arabic, putting my hand over my heart, too.

Lahsan didn't need one more job.

A few days into my stay, Sue had told me Lahsan lived in a small room on the top floor of the *riad*, which explained why he was at work day and night, pouring tea, hauling luggage up and down the stairs; serving breakfast first thing each morning and dinner to guests who decided to dine in each night. As I sipped strong coffee at a café on a square one afternoon, I saw Lahsan pulling suitcases from a taxi. I waved but it was crowded and I guessed he didn't see me because he didn't wave back. I watched him until he disappeared behind a wall, luggage and guests in tow, his stroll equal measures of determined and carefree.

◆ ◆ ◆

The sugar from the freshly poured mint tea sticks to my teeth and coats my tongue. Alone in the *riad's* courtyard, I hear the familiar call to prayer. It beckons five times a day from mosques and minarets, and it trickles in through the open roof, and slides down the blue and green Moorish tiles that cover the walls and floor. I let it finish, making a mental note to record it for my brother before I return to Europe the next day, then dash up to my room to grab a few things before heading out on my final night in Fez.

On the way back down, I see Lahsan talking to Sue at the bottom of the stairs. Gone are his leather slippers and the maroon-colored tunic he was wearing earlier, and in their place a red and blue soccer jersey, loose athletic shorts, long socks, and sneakers. I sit down on the stairs so we are eye to eye and smile, happy to see this boyish side of Lahsan. I ask him what he's up to.

"Playing soccer with my brother," he says, a smile carving its way across his mocha-colored cheeks.

He looks like any American boy back home, lighthearted and young, and reminds me of my brother and the neighbor boys he played with in our driveway.

Sue interjects, "Did you know Lahsan has an identical twin brother who also works here in the medina?"

Goosebumps prick my skin. I rest my chin in my hands, my elbows on my knees.

"No, I didn't," I say, staring at him.

I feel those invisible strings between us tighten.

"This might surprise you," I say trying to keep my voice from cracking. " But I, too, am a twin. I also have a twin brother."

Lahsan's grin spreads even wider. His eyes fill with comprehension and he puts his hand over his heart again, a gesture I've come to associate with him.

"Sister, now we are four in our family."

◆◆◆

In another courtyard that evening, a fountain bubbles and glows blue and green below an orange tree. The owner, Suzanna Clark, is also the author *A House in Fez*, a memoir recounting her purchase and restoration of her medina home, Riad Zany. She tells us she was presented with a scroll two-meters long, on it a list of names to which she and her husband, Sandy, added theirs as the newest proprietors. "It gave me the sense that we were merely custodians of the place, rather than owners," Suzanna said.

The weight of my own impermanence slowly seeps into the spaces between flesh and bone. In a place that has existed for over 1,000 years and will likely exist for 1,000 more, I, too, suddenly feel like a custodian of this miniscule moment in time. I'm just a small stone in my own history that will eventually turn to dust and blow away. This makes me think of something else. Another question I was asked once was whether twins die at the same time, too. "They come into the world together so I wondered if it was common for them to leave together," was the reasoning of the interrogator. I'd dismissed it as the stupidest thing I'd ever heard until later when I was alone with my brother and he told me he's always felt he'd never live beyond 50 years old.

Hairs tingled at the nape of my neck.

"That's *so* weird," I said to him. "I've always felt exactly the same way."

We both knew it wasn't so weird.

After dinner, I'm standing on the roof back at my *riad* when the mosques bellow their methodic hymn once again, calling the faithful from obscured passageways into streets I cannot see from my elevated position. The city's staggered skyline of cubes are topped with flat roofs that serve as both laundry rooms and playgrounds for the families that live below, as well as gardens for the bouquets of satellite dishes that sprout like sunflowers and beckon the outside world in. Only a week earlier, I'd thought the medina appeared dehydrated from a distance, void of life. But as with any place, just as with people, that which connects you is found deep below the surface.

Staring out over what I'd come to learn was a living and breathing city, the magnitude of the unseen and unknown overwhelms me, and I do the only thing I can think of. I take out my phone and record the sound of the *muezzin*'s haunting call to prayer so I can send it to my brother when he asks for it, which I know he will.

This story won a Silver Solas Award & was previously published in *Vignettes & Postcards from Morocco* (Reputation Books, 2016) & *The Best Women's Travel Writing, Vol. 11* (Travelers' Tales, 2017).

Old Bucket

ANN DUFAUX

Old black rubber bucket with handles—
today a donkey no longer carries you,
dripping with water,
from fountain to home.
Now deep in your heart,
geranium roots delve
and quench red blossoms' thirst.

Fez Medina Scaffolding
Photo by Siobhann Bellinger

A Jagged Edge in Fez

ERIN BYRNE

The medina is full of opportunities to practice compassion.
—Omar Chennafi, Moroccan photographer

"Wow, you must really love Morocco," a friend said to me recently.

I blanched. The thought of Morocco caused sharp rocks to skitter across my nerves as I recalled a strange episode that occurred on an earlier visit there.

◆ ◆ ◆

Sunlit dust motes descended in a hazy, late-afternoon slow dance, illuminating the ancient passageway of the Fez Medina as I stepped out of our *riad's* back door, following my friend Christina.

"Don't you remember?" Christina tossed over her shoulder. "You never said anything."

"Remember what?"

"I thought you just wanted to forget about it," Her voice took on that trembly tone we used when we gently exposed the other. "You like things, you know, nice."

An admission that I like things tidy appeared in my mind, but otherwise, nothing.

161

"Forget about *what*?"

◆ ◆ ◆

On my initial visit two years before that one, also with Christina, during my first hour in Fez, I had felt as if I were a paper doll swept along a crowd of *djellaba*-clad women, boys tumbling on each other's heels, laughing old men, bellowing donkeys, and beckoning shopkeepers. As the oldest walled city in the world, the Fez Medina is a narrow jumble of more than 9,000 pathways packed with a quarter of a million people.

As one who prefers an extra cushion of personal space, my senses were drenched and my balance teetered. I'd been flattened, and had ended up on my back, hyperventilating, on a bench in Café Clock: a multi-storied haven of quiet alcoves deep in the meandering medina.

I knew it would take an effort of will to become calm enough to be receptive to this chaotic place, so the next day, each time my body italicized itself, I softened: when the *muezzin's* call to prayer eerily invaded my dreams at 3:30 AM, I opened to allow its keening comfort to seep in; claustrophobic closeness of skin on skin, mingled breaths, and bodies pressing past in the souks caused an irrational electrical jolt on which I'd carefully lowered the voltage; and the sight of a white dog on its back, legs stiffly up, by the side of a road had sent a wave of revulsion through my veins, but I encouraged it to roll out.

My inner compass had sprung; it became clear that no map existed that could shed much light on this high-walled honeycomb of byways, crisscrosses, and dead ends. The instant I stepped out of our *riad's* door, I was lost. Helpless, I followed Christina's blond-haired lead and steered clear of the shadows.

I had never been in a place where a map would have been

obsolete and found it unnerving. No matter how many times we ventured out, the dusty ground twisted and turned in seemingly identical patterns, doors I'd noted as landmarks reappeared with disorienting regularity, and the concepts of north, south, east, and west evaporated. The only sight I recognized was the wooden front door of our *riad*—and only when it was inches from my nose.

I envisioned the medina from a higher perspective; from a helicopter above Fez, it would be tidier. I'd find a way to weave with ease among the hoards of humans, between walls lined like tall Crayola boxes full of multi-hued *babouche* slippers and layer upon layer of brightly woven rugs.

After a few days of trying this and every other trick in the book to sneak past my own self, the beauty of the medina had assuaged my auto-fears, and I finally experienced the essence of Fez—tasted tangy tagines, inhaled fresh lemons and mint, and jostled my way through the souks. Travel had become a way to both shrink and expand myself, and after that first trip to Fez, I felt as though my soul's sinews had been stretched and strengthened.

◆◆◆

My reverie was broken by Christina, who continued her reference to the earlier trip. "It was scary, all that blood. He was screaming."

I reached inward, grasping. Still nothing. Tried again.

In an instant, the twine that had held this memory in a tightly wound ball unraveled: a man in a filthy *djellaba* stood, arm out, gripping a shark-fin-sized shard of glass in his fist, its jagged edge dripping magenta onto his hand, his robe, the ground. Rivulets of blood ran down the side of his bald skull from an open gash on his temple. His eyes, light greenish-blue, expanded in terror. His wail spiraled up, an unceasing siren.

I checked my Technicolor memory with Christina. We had set out to find a shop where they made red fezzes, to purchase one for our friend. Rounding a corner, we'd nearly bumped into the man, staggering in his bloody stupor.

"He had a long face, high cheekbones, right?" I asked. "He zigzagged through the passageway, shrieking...he was tall, wasn't he? Off in the distance we could see those other guys running away?"

Yes, yes, yes. He'd left a crimson flower blossoming on the ground, yes, yes.

"I thought you just didn't want to talk about it," she said. "You *forgot?*"

When that image came careening out of the dark recesses of wherever I had imprisoned it, panic mushroomed inside my chest. I had memorized pages of notes from that trip and there was no mention of the man.

How could my mind cut a slice out of my experience and place it beyond my inner vision? In the intervening years, I'd sustained a serious concussion and recovered; had the scene of the screaming man spurted out of my head along with my own blood when I fell on a Paris street? Perhaps I'd held the image until only recently, as the stress of death and illness in my family crowded it out. Was my penchant for the nice keeping me inside a pristine palace where the pain of others or shocks to my system were locked outside the gates? Were my finely-tuned sensitivities guards who admitted only the acceptable?

What *else* in my life had I forgotten?

I had heard of mindfulness theories in which it was shown that our minds are constantly changing. This shift in thinking was what made travel so enticing to me. When I brushed up against the unknown in a foreign place, I discovered a world beyond my own expectations and had often felt transformed.

But I traveled *seeking* this change. I didn't want it

sneaking up on me.

This unexpected maneuver of my brain felt like a betrayal: I needed constant access to its files. Could it be that my mind was not a sunlit room lined with file-cabinets, but a labyrinth of sinister corners littered with sealed film canisters whose lids could pop off at any moment, unreeling scenes and images?

It was curious that I remembered the calls to prayer, the crowded souks, and the dead dog, but not the screaming man. Clearly, I had dissociated the trauma of that intimate moment in the alley, for one can rarely be closer to another human being than to be near them as they suffer. I'd refused this closeness by deleting the memory.

Christina and I had halted in shock, but the man ran off before we could offer him help or comfort him, touch his shoulder or hold his other hand. I felt guilty forgetting him; my self-protective padding had cut me off from reality as if I were a zombie, not fully alive.

As time has passed, I have thought of him often: his high, sharp cheekbones, his eyes wide in agony as he shrieked, the knuckles of his hand bulging as he squeezed the glass, a scarlet fountain spurting out, his bare, brown feet caked with gray dust. I wonder what his story was, where he is now. He has become in my mind more vivid and fully human in a way which is far beyond nice, and I feel connected to him in a three-dimensional way.

Perhaps the memory came rushing back two years later because by my second trip to Fez I had shoved a few of those cushions needed for personal space aside. The accident in Paris, the illness and death of loved ones, and perhaps most of all, the stretching effect of Morocco itself had cleared an internal space. My mind had held onto the scene until my spirit had expanded enough to take it in.

Perhaps we evolve as if in a widening spiral, the controls of our souls loosening with each outward wave of new realities, our inner world growing as our outer world includes more. Originally, Fez existed as two walled cities, built in 789 and 808. By the mid-11th century, the population had burgeoned, so the two towns were united with a single wall surrounding them. Just as the Medina's sandstone walls had extended to include more families, homes, and shops, my own boundaries had broadened.

Today, I consider my mind not a filing system or maze of creepy hiding places, but a place more like a foreign country. I am curious to discover what is in there. My question *What else have I forgotten?* has become *What will I remember next?* My energy has shifted from struggling to keep turmoil out, to holding open an inner door to let life in. Instead of scolding my brain, I try to cultivate a more welcoming spirit toward the unexpected, sometimes intrusive events of reality. I no longer wish to view from above, but to be immersed *in.*

◆ ◆ ◆

Each time I return to Fez, my anticipation is laced with awe, uncertainty, and the trepidation I've come to expect before encounters with that place of winding paths, close encounters, and surprises around every corner.

Do I love Morocco? I think of loves that I do have and see that they are ridged with rough contours: my sons are in their twenties and I still suffer anxiety when I imagine them driving, skiing, taking any risks. My father recently died, and time with my aging mother seems to tick like a runaway metronome. I adore so many people who live in faraway lands that my affection is often tinged with the searing sadness of missing them. Perhaps love requires that we clear an internal space for both joy *and* pain.

It is this that Morocco has taught me to do. The place that overwhelmed my mind into forgetting challenged it to remember. The chaos that chipped away at my protective padding brought bright markets, the soothing sounds of Arabic, and tea sweet enough to permeate my psyche and soften it.

So let the spiral of travel widen, let the compass quiver. For now, when I arrive in a place that overwhelms me, I watch for in-the-moment chances to cultivate compassion, and ready myself to sweep along on unpredictable currents that swell me, and to feel the untidy, soul-stretching, jagged edge of love.

This story won a Bronze Solas Award.

Babouches *in the Medina*
Photo by Ann Dufaux

Lost in the Medina, Poised to Make Another Faulty Choice

PAUL WASZINK

Three cats, one after the other, bounding along the right-hand wall (sliver of sunlight), to the next safe haven; a vendor of leather bags and wallets—bad teeth, deeply lined face—undecided about when to say "Welcome, Madame..." to Libby; a clot of a dozen Europeans, moving fast through this stretch (English? German?); two impossibly thin, impossibly leggy, tall Moroccan teenagers speeding through the streaming crowd like dolphins, chattering as they flit by on my left.

Haj telling a story at Café Clock in Marrakesh
Photo by Anna Elkins

Stepping Into the Story

STEFANIE HOFFMAN

So often, I find that traveling is a lot less about carefully planned itineraries and much more about learning how to step off a ledge without knowing how—or even if—you're going to land.

Like the time I went paragliding with a pilot in the Venezuelan Andes on a whim, and, as we were running to the edge of the cliff, suddenly started praying we would make it to the base of the mountain alive.

Or, more recently, like the first time I talked about mental illness to a room full of strangers at a café in the heart of Marrakesh. Had I thought too much about either adventure, I would have done neither. But in some ways, the latter was more terrifying.

Not that I thought about it at the time. The fact that I'd have to perform a story that would leave me vulnerable in front of a potentially harsh and critical audience seemed surreal and distant when I first embarked on the journey—like the inevitable cold splash that you shove to the back of your mind when you accept a double-dog dare to jump from the high-dive platform.

I was eager to step out of my frenetic, overcommitted life as a public relations professional to begin a 10-day writing and storytelling trek in Morocco because, well, it sounded like fun. Because it was a departure from a painful breakup and a job on the 39th floor of a San Francisco high-rise where I was putting in upwards of 60 hours week and still just scraping by.

After an excruciating, 18-hour, three-legged flight, I joined the 12-member writing group in Marrakesh. And a day later, we clambered aboard a bus bound for the village of Moulay Idriss. We were going to learn art of storytelling at the feet of Haj, one of the last remaining master Moroccan storytellers in the country, along with his small band of student apprentices who wanted to keep the tradition alive.

In Moroccan tradition, stories are primarily fables— usually fanciful narratives about princes who fall in love with fair maidens, poor villagers who find riches, and evil villains who get their come-uppances—told as a way to relay history, teach moral lessons to children, and pass on cultural beliefs that date back thousands of years.

By contrast, contemporary, American-style storytelling largely centers on intimate, real-life narratives that somehow change the storyteller or relay profound, personal growth.

Leading our daily writing workshops was Bay Area storyteller Doug Cordell, who helped guide us in both genres. Silver-haired and sardonic, Doug had a pedigree that included NPR's Snap Judgment, APM's Marketplace, and an array of local storytelling events. True to his American storytelling roots, his narratives were highly personal and darkly humorous—full of vengeful New York landlords or romantic interludes gone horribly awry—and his delivery always seemed to strike just the right balance of self-effacing humor and heart-rending vulnerability.

On the opposite side of this theater was Haj. It didn't matter that Haj told his tales in Arabic—his ability to bring ancient stories alive somehow transcended language and time and generations. Cloaked in a traditional red-and-gold *djellaba*, he told a story to our group. And as he spoke, his small, hunched frame suddenly seemed to become bigger with every wave of his cane and dramatic gesture of his arms, until he seemed to fill every corner of the room. Throughout the narrative, his undulating tone and facial expressions seamlessly transformed from wildly frightening to tranquilly joyful as he embodied the thieves and kings and magicians that pervaded his stories. I sat transfixed, forgetting that I couldn't understand a word. It didn't matter—Haj wasn't telling the story, he *was* the story.

I wanted to create a storytelling persona that blended Haj's theatrics and Doug's snarky candor. I wanted my story to be—big. Unforgettable. And yet, deeply relatable.

I did have a story like that. Five years prior, I experienced an attack on my life perpetrated by someone I knew, in my own two-bedroom, San Francisco apartment. My journey to heal prompted me to run to an island yoga retreat in Thailand only to realize that I couldn't orchestrate my own healing.

I had talked about it extensively with therapists, family, and friends—but never in public. Could I talk about it? It was both dramatic and intimate, so it checked off a lot of boxes.

But could I laugh about it? I'd think about that later.

Over Moroccan mint tea and spicy chicken tagine, I spent hours writing, rewriting, refining and, carving out themes on the rooftop garden terrace of our *riad*.

"'Beat out' your presentation," Doug instructed. "Most people hear things differently from the way they read or see them. So create three main points and stick to those."

Slow it down, he cautioned. Most people tend to speak faster when they get nervous, and in front of an audience, you're guaranteed to feel at least a few butterflies.

Reiterate your message, he told us. After taking your audience through your beats, you have to provide a sense of closure.

And if nothing else, be sure to have a strong ending and a strong beginning. That was most important.

Morning after morning, I took in a breath of sandalwood incense, gulped down my Turkish espresso, and scratched out what I had just written the evening before. Storytelling, I realized, was a completely different animal than writing. While we can follow relatively complex storylines in books and articles, we remember surprisingly few details when listening to an oral presentation. So where writing was florid and descriptive, storytelling was succinct and to the point. Where writing created mystique, storytelling pulled no punches. Where writing catered to the metaphor, storytelling illuminated the dramatic.

So I practiced, at night in my room. Over breakfast. In the *riad* lounge. I went over my notes, then flipped them over. I whispered my opening line as I meandered the cobbled alleys and fragrant markets of Moulay Idriss.

It wasn't until I looked out the train window at the brown and purple Atlas Mountains slowly diminishing against a beige desert landscape on the train back to Marrakesh that I realized the enormity of my undertaking; I was going to talk about mental illness to a room full of strangers.

I was going to open up about an event that was the source of PTSD, panic attacks, and countless nightmares from which I'd wake up screaming, my body drenched in sweat. A memory so painful that it still elicited feelings of emptiness and depression a good five years later.

I leapt up from my seat and found Doug in the adjacent train car, trying hard to breathe through the panic that was rising up in me like mercury in a thermometer. "I need to practice," I said. "I need to practice now."

Doug looked a little perplexed. "OK," he said. "Where do you want to go?"

"Anywhere."

The only place we could find to practice was in between

the cars, in front of the bathroom, over the rhythmic chugging of the train as it clattered over the rails. It would have to do.

"OK, take a deep breath. Start with your opening line," Doug said evenly.

I took a deep breath. "I ran away to an island yoga retreat in Thailand after an attack on my life by someone who wasn't quite a stranger," I began.

Stop. I was interrupted by a passenger entering the cramped, unisex bathroom.

Begin again. I forgot my transition to my first story beat. Stop.

Begin again. Again, I forgot the third beat.

"I don't think I can do this," I said. "I'm not ready."

Doug looked at me as if I just said I planned to throw myself off of the train. "What do you mean you can't do it? You'll be fine," he said, his New York accent accentuating each word.

Begin again. This time I made it to the end. I rolled through the next iteration without stopping. And the next one. "You're ready," Doug finally said.

At Café Clock that evening, I fidgeted nervously with my notes and crossed and uncrossed my legs as I watched my colleagues perform their stories, trying to focus on what they were saying. I was the next to the last one in the lineup.

Of course, I had come this far. I couldn't back down now, I told myself. But that wasn't true. I could have insisted on not performing that night. No one would have minded—not even Doug.

Maybe I choose to go right up to the edge for a reason—because a part of me knows that I'm able to take the next step, even if there's no discernable ground on which to stand. Even if I'm terrified of what's next. And the panic that precedes the fall is just a desperate attempt to hold onto a path that's comfortable and familiar, even if it's outlived its usefulness. Even if I've outgrown the direction it's taking me.

Erin, our other writing instructor, introduced me to the audience. "Stefanie Hoffman is now going to perform 'The Healing Road.'"

I stepped up to the center of the room. Both the main room and the balcony were full, packed with Moroccan storytellers, a long table of British tourists and of course, a dozen of my writing colleagues—all waiting for me to start. Instead of the noise of the train, I would be speaking over the sound of chatter, the clanking of dishes, and the whirring of the espresso maker.

I was ready to tell this story.

I looked down and whispered my first line. I looked up and faced my audience. Then I took a deep breath and a step forward.

The Roman ruins of Volubilis
Photo by Siobhann Bellinger

We Are Here Now: Moulay Idriss

CHANT THOMAS

Everyone else has departed for the day's activities, leaving us alone in the sweetness of solitude. Bahaar sits near me, knitting bright red yarns for Zakia's hat, now and then sharing a poem she has brought forth from the rich vault of silence.

In the absence of chatter and the swirling energies of our traveling companions, another reality flows more easily and completely into our consciousness, especially up here on the rooftop terrace, where the soft breeze sets the short bamboo dancing, a hammock sways empty—holding still-lingering perfumes of its last inhabitant. Little chirps of sparrows float by in the morning breeze, followed by the clapping of flapping wings as a flock of pigeons lifts off a nearby rooftop. Suddenly the loudest sounds—of braying donkeys urgent with fear—rise from the square far below where veterinarians conduct the donkey clinic.

Then the donkeys stop braying and a few dogs begin barking, perhaps wondering what all the fuss could be about.

Houses here in the ancient medina crowd together, wall to wall, climbing three, four, and more stories up the steep mountainside from their tiny lots, reaching skyward to accommodate large families where young adults typically live at home until leaving for marriage. Sounds of living close together come and go like the white clouds traveling the blue sky. Infants cry, toddlers wail, children chatter and scream with delight. Adults speak in subdued tones, raising voices to make a point.

A few rooftops away, a woman hangs laundry, all but her face and hands covered by her *hijab* and *djellaba*. She looks this way, notices I am watching and continues with her work, absorbed by her thoughts or prayers; I can't even guess.

Behind her rooftop, houses drop down the mountain, then disappear behind the steep slopes that soften into rolling hills covered with olive groves and laced with small rivers. On the last hill before the valley flattens into vast verdant plains, the ancient Roman ruins of Volubilis rise—all its arches, columns, and crumbling walls casting their shadows. Beyond all this, distant mountains cradle the azure sky, launching legions of white clouds that will arrive here at this rooftop sometime later this morning.

More voices rise from warrens of narrow walkways and fountain squares far below, joining with voices emanating from the adjoining houses. Many words, phrases and sentences of conversation, all in Darija, completely unintelligible to me, yet clearly conveying the most basic message: I am here, right now, in Morocco!

Moulay Idriss
Photo by Tim Daw

The King's Room

JEAN-BERNARD PONTHUS

Here is the King's room: five-meters wide by six-meters long and seven-meters high. Square tiles shining in navy blue and white patterns. Stained-glass windows shedding hues on the floor. Robust wooden ceiling beams carved and painted.

A discussion occured before entering it. *Is the foreign guest entitled to inhabit such room?* The caretaker was not in favor of it. But the lady in charge of welcoming the group in Moulay Idriss, the holy city of Morocco, forced him to give the room to the foreign guest.

"It was booked in advance," she argued. "You promised he would have it," she said, this time switching to Arabic.

The caretaker of Dar Ines was reluctant to be bullied by a Western lady, even if she had been living for eight years in his country and had mastered his language.

I tried my best to ease the caretaker, using my French, the vernacular language of Morocco. "Will I have the big room, Sir?" I asked, unsure of what this room represented to him.

He yielded to the pressure.

I'm in.

Meanwhile, the other guests have been shown their rooms.

My door is ajar. One of them peeks in. She is amazed at the beauty of it. She goes directly toward the windows, opens the wooden shutters frenetically to see the view. The fresh air breezes in deep. She is struck by the space in front of her: hills covered in bright white cube houses. Down the street are visible arcades composed of 200 meters of white, curved Arabic arches—a scene that could have been lifted directly from the 1910 paintings of Albert Marquet on his trip to Morocco. It was, without doubt, a room with a view.

"How come you got the room?" she asks, with no intention of budging.

Apparently, her room is a mere cupboard with no window. Just my three big beds alone would be twice the surface area of her room. Indeed, I have no title of property for this room. But I don't want to get expelled from it.

So, I say loudly and mightily: "I am the King."

I crown myself like Napoleon did on the coronation day, leaving the pope alone and unattended.

"I'm the King of this room," I repeat fiercely.

The other two guests of the house, hearing the coronation process, pop in. They, too, are struck by its grandeur and charm. Their rooms are clearly not equal to mine: dark, without any ornamentation, a single bed among a void space—like a prison cell for a tycoon on an Asian island.

The discrepancy is huge and charged, recalling luxury versus poverty, articulate versus analphabet, business seats versus economy seats, yellow vests versus Parisians!

The next morning at breakfast, the issue is raised again.

"Why such a room for a self-crowned King?"

"Did he win the lottery to get this room?"

The plebs are plotting a revolution ahead. After all, kings can be beheaded, especially in an old continent, say these folks from the New World. And approaching the King's room, as in Versailles, is a privilege not everyone can get.

Allah is almighty, but a king must have soldiers to protect him. Yet in the room he stays alone—even as he sees the rebellion coming and growing, like the ebbs and flows of his unknown territories. So, he needs to gain time. Strategically, he tries to play the enemies against one another.

"Who shall get the room first?" he asks, hoping to create division amongst the rebels.

Old techniques always work.

But to calm down further rebellion, he says, "You guys should have it when I leave."

Retreat is always the best option to gain time.

Next, he tries to point out the drawbacks of his kingdom: no privacy, noise coming in all night from the street, sleep deprivation. He depicts the drawbacks with exaggerated and unfair observations, but then stops. Should he do too much, his whole strategy will collapse like a castle of cards.

Then he conjures up the figure of the caretaker. "You should bribe him," he insists. "You didn't know you have to tip the guy?" he adds arrogantly, showing off his superiority to the ignorant plebs.

His ploy is working. The rebels start figuring out how much money they should pour into the caretaker's hand to get the room. The King entices them to spend a huge amount in order to ruin them, as if he were competing at an auction battle without having the proper funds. It works marvelously. They start greasing the cartetaker's palm. Quickly and wisely, the King goes and fetches the police to witness the corruption ahead.

Arrested, the rebels now spent their nights in jail without noticing any difference from their previous rooms because they once again found a single bed with nothing around.

At last, the King is secured and keeps his kingdom for at least 1,001 nights.

Rose Button on "Donkey Day" in Moulay Idriss
Photo by Tim Daw

Donkey Day Song

MARSHA DALTON (WITH DICK DALTON)

This is a story of compassion for animals. In 1927, a American traveler named Amy Bend Bishop took pity on the poor, overworked donkeys of Morocco and established the American Fondouk, a free veterinarian service in Fez for donkeys, mules, and horses.

More recently, a New Zealander named Rose Button waded through the government application process to create "Donkey Day" in the nearby village of Moulay Idriss. The Fondouk vets come to the village from Fez once a month to treat the donkeys and mules there.

Visiting Moulay Idriss on a tour, I was awed by the work of these compassionate people. Some lyrics started kicking around in my mind. Then this song was born.

My husband, Dick Dalton, helped on the vocals.

◆ ◆ ◆

Verse 1:

A donkey's life is hard in Morocco
We carry big loads where the cars can't go
A thousand loads I've hauled up and down these stairs
I'd like to think maybe somebody cares

Dar Zerhoune is OK
I love to see Miss Rose on Donkey Day.

Verse 2:

I go to Moulay Idriss on Donkey Day
Us donkeys and mules hee-haw and br-a-a-ay
The vets check me out to see if I'm OK
They give me vitamins and a snack of hay
        Only sixty dollars from the USA
        Covers fifty donkeys on a Donkey Day.

Verse 3:

They call me Donkey Number twenty-three
My man says you don't name a tax-i
He loads me down with such heavy packs
I feel it in my legs and in my back
        Stick me with a needle, take away my pain
        Treat my saddle sores and send me off again.

Verse 4:

A certain mule needed a special test
They put him in a truck and took him off to Fez
He had a bad limp before he went away
The next time I saw him, he was all OK
        The Fondouk vets are my heroes
        They make our lives better in Mo-rocco.

Verse 5:

I may have a pessimistic attitude
But think of all the things us donkeys do
I'm the backbone of this economy [get it?]

My man needs to take good care of me
        Once a month in the Moulay
        Hear us donkeys bray on Donkey Day.

Verse 6:

Now donkeys and mules come from far away
We like our men to hear what the wise vets say,
"You want a healthy donkey, not one that's sick?
Then take it easy, Donkey Man, with that stick
        Allah will look down and smile on you
        If you're kind to your donkey friend too
        Let him drink water all along the way
        Take him to the Moulay on Donkey Day."

Verse 7:

The men learn that Donkey Day is good for them
Vets helping donkeys helps the men
"Give your little donkey a day of rest
The donkey will feel that she is blessed
        Munchin' in a field of grass all day long
        Maybe she'll sing a little donkey song."
        Only sixty dollars USA
        Helps a lotta donkeys on Donkey Day.

Photo by Siobhann Bellinger

Stepping Through

HUDSON LINDENBERGER

As I sucked the cool, sweet air into my lungs, I paused for a moment. I could feel my heart pounding out a staccato beat from deep within my chest. A thin sheen of sweat covered my face, and a slightly damp streak ran down the center of my back. I had been following the ever-climbing pathways in this city for the last 20 minutes, and I knew I needed to sit down for a moment.

Off to my left, a riot of colorful tiles captured my interest. They were covering three broad steps that led to yet another pathway. I walked over and sat down on them. It felt good to relax. I swung my bag off my back and pulled out my water bottle. As I sipped the liquid and felt my blood calm back down, something out of the corner of my eye caught my attention.

It was a long passageway shrouded in darkness. On both sides of it, mud and brick buildings towered high, each one leaning drunkenly upon its neighbor. It seemed that little light ever brightened the cobbles that lined the road. At the end, I could make out the shape of a massive keyhole doorway wreathed in white marble. Its immense wooden doors were flung open, revealing a lovely courtyard with a fountain bubbling in the middle of it. I felt myself being drawn toward the doorway.

Just then the distinctively lonely cry of a *muezzin* rang

out, calling the faithful to afternoon prayer. On the heels of his cry, another and yet another voice joined him from the minarets sprinkled across this hilltop city. Their buzzing cries shook me out of my trance and brought me back to my senses.

What was I thinking? Walking unannounced into someone's home is never a good idea, especially here in the Muslim holy city of Moulay Idriss Zerhoun, deep in the Atlas Mountains, in the country of Morocco.

But, I wanted to step through that doorway, to see what was hidden behind it, to meet the people who called it home.

I have always been drawn to doorways. There is something about them that speaks to my soul—the chance to step through a portal and instantly be transported to a different place, a different adventure. In Prague, I once went from a rainy, gloomy evening to a room full of light and joy, filled with folks hoisting beers and singing songs. Escaping the heat once in the Florida Keys, I found myself hearing stories of the sea from old salts just because I ducked into a room. Even as a kid, I was prone to wander off into different rooms looking for something to capture my overactive mind.

From the moment I stepped off the plane five days ago in the city of Fez, I knew that this country was trouble for me. There were the massive gateways into the ancient warren of the medina, the beating heart of the city—a place with enough passageways and doorways to keep me happy for decades. Inside the city, I saw doors of every size. Some stood ten-feet tall surrounded by elaborate woodwork and tiles that took my breath away, and other tiny ones surely led to that mythical land where Alice escaped after following the rabbit.

I spent every day wandering the city in a euphoric daze, excited as to what I would stumble onto next. When the time came for my group to head deeper into the country toward Moulay Idriss Zerhoun, I felt the familiar churn of emotions that most travelers feel. I was excited to see what awaited me down the road, but also sad to be leaving a place that had captured my heart so quickly.

As we climbed deeper into the mountains, I wondered about what was next. How would Moulay possibly match the chaotic splendors of Fez? Granted, the city had only started letting non-Muslims stay overnight in 2005. Even from far away, I could smell the mystery surrounding it.

After several hours in the car, I caught my first glimpse of the city. From across a valley filled with farms and groves of olive trees, it beckoned like an oasis. White, red, and green roofs topped rows upon rows of white houses, each level stacked higher and higher until it topped off the rocky protrusions that the city perched upon.

As we neared the city, our guide told us we would have to walk in; no cars were allowed nor could they fit through the tight byways of the ancient city. As we entered the first city doorway, I felt that familiar twinges of excitement. What was behind it? What could I find here?

Climbing to our *riad* hotel, we were passed by the locals' vehicle of choice: donkeys loaded with baskets of figs and firewood. Unlike Fez, the residents of Moulay Idriss Zerhoun love to paint the outsides of their houses. Aqua greens gave way to vibrant reds. Turning a corner, I saw that all of the stairs ahead of me were painted a different color. This city was a contrast to Fez, where thousands upon thousands of people live seemingly on top of each other. Here life seemed more relaxed. The people smiled and waved to me as we walked by.

Once we checked in, I headed out armed with my bag and camera. I had no plan; I only knew that I wanted to go deeper into the city. Unlike the twisting and turning pathways of Fez, where you can easily lose your way, navigating this city was relatively easy. Rounding one turn, I came across the huge entryway to the main mosque with its doors flung wide. Inside, the remains of the city's namesake are buried: the great-grandson of the Prophet Muhammad, making this spot one of the holier ones in the Muslim world. The portal pulled at the edges of my heart. But I only made it part way before a long wooden pole barricaded the entrance, stopping me in my tracks. A battered, rusting sign informed me that only Muslims might continue forward, that this way was barred to me. I marveled at the brilliant white tiles and tower soaring upward ahead of me, but I knew I must turn back. With one last glance, I turned and retraced my steps.

Back at the entrance, I chose a winding road that disappeared under a large archway leading upwards. As I climbed, I paused to look at the beautiful doorways lining it. There were huge brass knockers in the shape of hands, wooden doors studded with metal rivets pounded in decades ago, decrepit ones that looked like they might fall off at any time. The stories they must have. Toward the top was where I saw the passageway.

As I sat there listening to the fading cries of the *muezzin*, a silence seemed to settle over me. It was a feeling of contentment, of feeling fulfilled. I felt a stillness instead of the wanderlust that usually defines me. Over the last week, I had mingled with the residents of this country, haggled with merchants over a few cents, laughed at their jokes, and listened with rapt attention to storytellers weaving their tales of mystery. But now I enjoyed the peacefulness of this spot.

I leaned back on the wall behind me, took another sip of my water, and shut my eyes, reveling in the moment.

A short while later, I heard a sound from my left. I opened my eyes and looked down the passageway. A young woman in a beautiful robe and *hijab* had come to the entrance of the gate. She looked directly at me, and our eyes locked for a few seconds. She shyly smiled, nodded, and then grabbed the edges of the door to pull it closed. I smiled to myself and looked around. The road I had been following ended only a few feet from where I stood, but there were two other pathways leading in opposite directions off of it. I stood up, swung my bag back on my back, and headed toward them. It was time to continue onward.

Exploring the Edge: Moroccan Confessionals

KYLE KEYSER

Tuesday, April 7th, Fez Medina

The bathroom mirror was a small, jeweled rectangle on a green-tiled wall. Framed inside it was me: a white, 40-something, gay American male with a healthy libido and a propensity for trouble. I cocked my head to the side and ran my fingers through my hair, messing it up just right. I was getting ready to meet a Moroccan stranger named Khalid.

My phone vibrated and I looked down. The message read, "I'm parked at mosque. Right by Blue Gate."

Oh shit, we're driving somewhere? A little jolt raced up my spine. *I thought the hotel bar was in walking distance.* I squinted at myself in the mirror. *Do I really want to do this?* My *riad* was dark, and the group I was traveling with long asleep. There was no one to tell in case I turned up dead.

As I considered the consequences, the hum of the ancient Fez Medina wafted in through the small window just above my shower. It played on my senses, like a sly genie inviting me to follow. I turned off the light and stepped out onto narrow streets that told stories of risk and reward: the bloodied, severed goat heads alongside hot plates of meat, so rich they make your mouth water; or the soprano cries of one-eyed kittens, lost amongst the steps of giants. I brushed past them in the crowd and, like thumpers in an old pinball machine, they propelled me toward the exit.

Khalid was waiting by the gate as I emerged. We exchanged shy smiles. I got in the passenger seat of his car and, with the click of the seatbelt, buckled in.

Monday, April 8th, On the Road

"As long as you have me in Casablanca by 10 AM on Thursday, we're good."

He nodded quickly as if to say "no problem." With that, I surrendered to a road trip with Khalid.

Fifty-kilometers later, we're bee-lining it for the Rif Mountains of northern Morocco. Khalid is dodging dogs and men in dusty *djellabas*. I'm taking pictures and playing Passenger Seat DJ.

"Today you learns something about Morrr-occo," he says.

I smiled and retorted, "Today you learn something about American country music."

"Yes, aye all-rrready know Dolly Parrr-ton. Aye loves her."

"Yeah, well you know shit about the Dixie Chicks."

A twangy violin fills the car. He turns up the volume. We pass a street sign, written mostly in Arabic, that shows north for Chefchaouen. He points, talking over the music, "We'll be there in a thh-ree hours." I give him the "thumbs up" and settle back into my seat.

Cowboy, take me away.

Tuesday, April 9th, Chefchaouen

How cute. He's reminding me to pray.

I clicked off the lights and quickly climbed back into

bed. Khalid and I adjusted ourselves to each other's outline and, in a sleepy, thick accent he said again, "Do not forrr-get to make all-ahh."

Earlier that day, he told me what the five-pointed star represented on the Moroccan flag. He said each point was a reminder to acknowledge Allah as a prophet of the one true God, to pray, to give to the poor, to practice Ramadan, and to not worship false prophets.

How cute, I thought. *He's bringing it full circle.*

I collected the day's gratitudes and sent small prayers to the heavens. When I finished, I turned and whispered to him, "OK. I prayed." Khalid twitched a little as if I woke him in the middle of a dream.

"Great... as you like," he yawned. "But pla-ease no a-sleeping late tomorrow. We gets up at 9 o'clock for brrr-eakfast." He goes to turn over. "So please, I ask again, do not forrr-get to make all-arm."

Wednesday, April 10th, Tangier

Khalid handed me a banana as we entered the land-side entrance of Hercules' Cave. He told me, "Here, this is good for-rr you. It help make you healthy and strong." *Fun timing*, I thought.

The story goes that Hercules slept in this cave, located on Morocco's Atlantic coast near Tangier, before embarking on his eleventh labour. After a good night's sleep, he decided to smash his way there instead of crossing the mountains, thus creating the Strait of Gibraltar and connecting the Atlantic Ocean to the Mediterranean Sea.

A unique feature of the cave is that its second entrance looks like Africa. Looking out from the inside, you can see it. I asked Khalid to stand in front of it, sort of pensive-like, so that I could get a picture. He obliged. It was the perfect opportunity to ditch that fucking banana.

We pulled into the departure lane of the Casablanca Mohammed V International Airport and approached the terminal. Khalid and I were both quiet. I squinted through the morning sun, watching a bustle of cars compete for the curb, while he pulled past them to the Air France drop-off point. As he came to a stop, I looked at my phone. 7:53 AM. We made it. Just like he said.

"You will have a-plenty time to go," he said as he motioned toward the terminal doors.

I looked in the direction of his gesture and saw a family walking their bags through the parted doors. "I can't thank you enough. It was really great."

"Yes. It was very nice."

"I know we can't exactly start making out or anything."

Khalid smiled. "No."

"But…" I extended my hand and he took it. His grip was subtle and warm. "Thank you. I saw so much I wouldn't have seen otherwise."

He squeezed. "Yes. And me too."

After a pause, I released his hand and unclicked my seatbelt. Khalid reached into the backseat and, before I was able to go, said, "Here." He handed me another banana. *Again with the banana.* "Be good and take a-care of yourrr-self." I grabbed it and he held on. We shared a moment of extended gaze while both holding onto the elongated fruit.

"I know we can't kiss each other," I fought a smirk that badly wanted free. "But I don't think this is much better."

Moulay Idriss
Photo by Keiko Moriyama

View Panoramic

KEIKO MORIYAMA

I eagerly followed three boys, who were no older than eight or nine, up the steep, uneven stairway bordered by walls of white and turquoise blue. Skeletal cats pranced in and out of nooks and crannies along the narrow pathway. Whiffs of freshly diced chilies and spicy curry pastillas permeated the warm, humid air. The young boys said they would show me a place called View Panoramic. I was curious.

I stayed in the holy town of Moulay Idriss during a week-long travel writers workshop led by Tim Cahill. I'm not sure what made me sign up for the workshop. Morocco was neither at the top of my destination list, nor was I a writer. But I desperately wanted to retire, and had a dreamy desire to one day write travel stories to share with anyone interested in reading them. As I sat in Tim's workshop every morning with twelve accomplished travel writers, I kept asking myself, "What the hell am I doing here?"

Moulay Idriss sits on two hills at the base of Mount Zerhoun, and from a distance looks much like two giant snow globes glistening in the sun, surrounded by green cascading valleys. The town is named after Moulay Idriss el Akhbar, a man credited for bringing Islam to Morocco, and who is buried in the mausoleum inside the town mosque. Up until 2005, the town itself was off-limits to non-Muslims. Even today, the infrastructure for tourism is almost nonexistent with only a handful of guesthouses and eateries. We stayed at Dar Zerhoune, a guesthouse conveniently situated near the center of town.

The writing workshops were held in the mornings, giving us afternoons to wander the town's maze-like passageways. The central plaza, surrounded by tiny shops and food vendors, teemed with colorfully-dressed women carrying bags of groceries, hurried men parading by with large bundles of produce on their backs, and screaming school children playing tag. I often sat at the plaza café sipping on hot mint tea, chatting with the local high school kids wanting to practice their English, or watching the donkeys clip-clopping by with their loaded panniers. In the evenings, I lounged at the rooftop restaurant of our guesthouse with a glass of wine enjoying the sunset. In the distance, I could hear the melodic chanting of prayer calls. With each passing day, I fell in love with the pace and rhythm of Moulay Idriss.

As we neared the hilltop, the boys turned and grinned at me, pleased with their momentary triumpth. "Look. This is the View Panoramic," said one of the boys as he gestured to his left. I turned the corner to see what he was pointing at, and my jaw dropped. I couldn't move. "Oh my god, this is magnificent," I whispered. Two hundred yards from where we were standing was a hill sprayed with hundreds of white and crème-colored dwellings against a backdrop of luminous jade valleys. Nestled toward the bottom of the hill stood the illustrious mosque covered with shimmery green tiles. The View Panoramic was impossibly gorgeous and sent chills up my spine. It reminded me of my first glimpse of Machu Picchu at sunrise or the time I first felt the showery mists of the thunderous Iguazu Falls. Both were moments of sheer exhiliartion. The View Panoramic gripped me in the same way.

The hordes of tourist buses have not yet discovered Moulay Idriss. I hope they never will.

Traveling Haiku on the Road in Morocco

CHANT THOMAS

Doors open. Doors close,
sometimes with hand on the knob.
Open book. Turn the page.

On the road again.
Push the boundaries beyond.
Expand horizons.

Depart, then arrive.
Settle into a new place.
Start again. Repeat.

Clouds obscure the view.
Watch for what transpires behind
that which appears. Look!

These poems appeared on the *Deep Travelogue* blog.

Six Scribbles on Birch Bark

BONNIE FLADUNG

Scribble One: A haiku. Find the perfect piece of birch bark. Maybe it's silver and flat, or scrolled with curly edges. You'll know the one. Write a haiku to the season or a poem about nature.

> Birch tree sheds its bark
> Scraps of white midst fallen leaves
> Pages of my life

Scribble Two: A bookmark. Sketch a flower, or a feather, or a stick figure dancing in flames. Light the fire to pick up a book and turn the page, take flight from reality, disappear into the fragrance of words.

Scribble Three: A list. The earliest birch-bark manuscripts were discovered in Russia at Novgorod. Thousands of texts. Not profound literary works but letters and lists, edicts and alphabets. Bullet point the details of your everyday life:

- Recipes and groceries
- Books to read and fantasies
- Garden seeds and beds to weed
- Ideas and epiphanies

Scribble Four: A map. Draw a rough sketch with charcoal and pin it to your door.

"Gone fishing. Follow the path round the garden, beyond the gazebo, into the woods and down the bank. You will find me in the brook, with my pole and waders. 'X' marks the spot."

Scribble Five. An invitation. Inscribe your request in shimmery teal ink:

"Come to my tea party, and wear your maddest hat. We'll dine under the leafy canopy, sipping sweet nectar from china teacups, surrounded by hummingbirds dashing for gold."

Scribble Six. A canoe. Soak the bark to soften, then cut-bend-and-shape. Whip stitch the seams with sweet grass, and seal with sap or pine pitch. Pen your haiku on the bow in waterproof ink. Captain it with an acorn and add a pebble for balance. Float the story of your life down the river, watching it bob and twist out of control, around a bend and out of sight.

Moroccan Zellij
Photo by Anna Elkins

Finding Home

MICHELLE ZEIDMAN

I glide in my long skirt down a dark, tight lane. I pass a lilac-colored playground with painted tires and a blue slide. I arrive at an ancient door with a heavy brass ring. I clank the knocker three times, and my call is returned by a tumble of footsteps falling down a worn, cobblestone path.

Inside: beige, water-stained walls. Underfoot: green and white tiles in a herringbone pattern. I smell mold and damp and centuries of prayer. In a dark alcove, I see a plush, red velvet Torah cover embroidered with musty gold thread and Hebrew characters I cannot read. I feel sad and wobbly in this place. I wish my grandfather where here to guide me through the history. Instead, it's a Moroccan man in a heavy wool coat who opens the door, motions me around the vacant synagogue, and leaves me to absorb the past.

Jews have long left Fez's *mellah*—its historic Jewish quarter. It's now inhabited by Muslims whose homes overlook the Jewish cemetery and abut this old synagogue. In Fez, like so many other places, Jews have been persecuted. It's in our blood to be driven out of our homes, made to be "other," and unwelcome in places that were once ours.

Still, I feel well-received here in Morocco, and every *salaam* is returned: by the man on the train who pauses from watching me paint to silently observe the call to prayer, by the new friend who dresses me in her finest *takchita*, and by the fat lady in dirty undies who scrubs me raw with mud in the public *hammam*—or bathhouse.

Morocco wraps me in its nest of twisty byways and orange trees. It beckons me with its carefully laid *zellij* tiles and countless feral cats. It calls me home to a land I'm not from, to an abandoned synagogue with signs I cannot understand, to a locale apart from time, to a place my grandpa's spirit lurks. I am once again connected to my roots.

This vignette appeared on the *Deep Travelogue* blog.

In the Medina

ALLISON RENWICK

In the medina, I am a coiling ribbon of flypaper. Everything sticks to me. I'm wrapped in sensations, I am sensations.

In the medina, I am a strip of flypaper studded with skittering cats, lurching donkeys, ricocheting children bouncing off grannies and onto my arms, my feet.

In the medina, I am a band of flypaper bound up in sounds, "*Bonjour* Madame, tannery this way," clatter of hooves, clang of metal, scrape of broom, shuffle of slippered feet.

In the medina, I am flypaper peppered with the blue patterns of ceramics, red and gold of knotted rugs, dots of colored beads, filigrees of silver, dull black of recycled rubber, bright brass of tea pots.

In the medina, I am a ribbon of flypaper, trapped in my sticky self-containment, recoiling inward for refuge, bits of this place forever with me.

Photo by Ann Dufaux

Step Back in Time

ANN DUFAUX

Doors open like magic during my short stay in Morocco: blue doors, brown doors, multi-colored doors with intricate vegetation and flower designs. Almost all have hinges in the shape of the hand of Fatima, to protect the people within from what Moroccans refer to as the "evil eye"—or destructive stares that can bring illness and misfortune. A friend explains that there is an old saying—*khamsa fi ainek*—and it means *five fingers in your eye*. "With that symbol, harmful people will be turned away from their threshold and their loved ones kept safe," she says.

I wander down the narrow winding streets of the medieval medina. Grey, tan, drab yellow walls tower four to five stories aboveground. High up, a few tiny barred windows puncture the walls here and there. I wonder: *Is that all the light the people living within get?*

Shade must be precious in the dog days of summer. Guidebooks say it gets terribly hot, but I'm visiting in early March and the weather is temperate.

The byways in the medina are so narrow that it's hardly possible for two people to walk abreast. A man approaches with a three-wheel pushcart loaded with fruits and vegetables and bounces down wide steps: plunk, plunk, plunk. He cries "*Balak!*" and I move out of his way, hold my breath, press my back into the wall, and let him through

Goods are not only carried in carts. A donkey approaches too, its saddlebags loaded with six large bottles of propane gas. A man with a warm smile invites me out of the way inside his workshop where he embroiders elaborate caftans with silver thread. I bend my head and step in. After the donkey passes, I turn to leave and ask for directions. "The souk, please?" The man points toward the market. "Left, then right, then left again. Keep going down. You can't miss it. "*Inshallah!*" I utter, feeling grateful.

The medina is a maze that I'll have to learn to navigate. All the passageways seem alike. No street signs with names show the way, and even if there were any, it would be difficult to decipher the Arabic.

I follow the tailor's instructions. Crowds of women and men come up from the Bab R'Cif gateway to the medina. Other shoppers stream in from quieter lanes that feed into the large, noisy main thoroughways of the souk. The lanes of the medina are like the tiny lines in the palm of my hand that join the larger vertical lines. The larger lines—the "life line" and the "heart line"—would be the Talaa Khebira, and Talaa Seghira, the famous wide and narrow main streets of the medina.

◆ ◆ ◆

It's still early morning when I arrive at the market, and it is still all hustle and bustle. The small shops have opened for the day. The owners are hawking their wares on Talaa Seghira where it's mostly handcrafts: *babouche* slippers in dozens of stunning colors, an array of tagine dishes, simple clothes, and fancy garb for special occasions. On Talaa Khebira, it's mostly food. You find live fowl and pigeons pecking the ground, rabbits in cages nibbling cabbage leaves and carrot peels. A hen clucks, a rooster crows. A woman selects the latter and a tall, bearded man steps forward and grasps the squawking bird by the neck. He chops off its head with a sharp knife and swiftly de-feathers the creature before handing it over in a bag to the woman. Back in our western world, we can forget that meat comes from a living animal. Our cuts come tidy and prepared in plastic wrap. But here most people don't have refrigerators. The passage from life to death is quick and straightforward.

I keep walking downhill and notice oranges and lemons piled high at one stall and, right after, another man selling olives, pickled vegetables, nuts, almonds, and dried fruit. Before reaching a street cart further on, it's easy to guess which fragrant herbs permeate the air without even seeing them first. There has to be cilantro and parsley. But then the overwhelming scent of fresh mint leaves soon drowns all else out, and a mound of literally hundreds of crisp green bunches appears. My mouth waters at the thought of last night's hot mint tea, a greeting token from the host at the *riad*.

I head toward the guesthouse, needing a rest after the long walk and all the pleas of merchants everywhere trying to sell me their goods. I've learned to turn them away by saying *"La shukran,"* no thank you.

Getting my bearings, I walk by the impressive doors of one of the larger mosques I noticed earlier. It is now open. Men are kneeling on prayer mats. I pass by, having been forewarned: non-Muslims are forbidden access. I will not enter.

I reach the place where my friends and I are staying, press the buzzer, and wait. In a few minutes. Lahsan, with his broad smile, lets me in. The hallway leads to the ground floor inner patio. It's amazing how much sunlight streams down from the open roof above. At midday there is no need for electricity.

"Would you like me to bring you a glass of mint tea up

on the terrace?" Lahsan asks. "What a wonderful idea!" I say as I follow him three flights up. Each beautifully tiled step is high, and I gasp for air as I reach the top. How amazing to be in the heart of the old city with its jagged layout of flat roofs staggered uphill and downhill everywhere one looks. I sink into soft cushions on a wrought iron chair, lift my glass of hot tea from a beautiful table with its intricate *zellij* mosaic patterns of white, blue, green, and purple colors. Sipping my tea, I soak it all in. Screeching swallows are flying low above the rooftops while a woman hangs out her wash on a clothesline nearby. Cats tightrope from rooftop to rooftop and, just then, a white one leaps one foot lower. All is quiet…

…until I hear a chant, issuing loud and clear from a nearby mosque. An *imam*. His voice is followed by a voice echoing, then another and another, from minaret to minaret. Throughout the city, others lift their voices in prayer. It's midday in ancient Fez.

My heart beats faster. The hi-tech world I live in back in France claims that we are in the golden age of interconnectedness—despite all conflicts around the globe.

Although Fez is not my home, its old rhythms make me feel somehow more connected—to a deeper place where I feel a sense of belonging, of roots, of ancestry.

This story was longlisted for the 2015 Fish Publishing Short Story Contest.

Cat in the Fez Medina
Photo by Siobhann Bellinger

Hamza's tools at Craft Draft, Fez Morocco
Photo by Anne Sigmon

Seeking the Center

ANNE SIGMON

Take a step away from yourself—and behold—the Path!
—Abu Sa'id Ibn Abi'l Khayr 10th-century Sufi poet

A heavy, hand-forged compass and a ruler lay on the front table. "These are the most important instruments of craftsmanship—the tools we use to find the center."

The speaker was Hamza El Fasiki, a craftsman and champion for the renowned Moroccan crafts community— metal workers, wood carvers, bookbinders, ceramicists, tanners and dyers—that has thrived in the ancient city of Fez, Morroco, for a thousand years.

My ten travelmates and I had squeezed onto wood benches and stools in his cramped artist studio in one of the oldest sectors of Fez to learn more about the city's craft traditions and the 21st-century pressures facing their community.

Through the open window, I heard the muffled sound of a radio tuned to Arabic music and the staccato tap-tap-tapping of a coppersmith at work.

Hamza's studio walls were lined with hand-made tools— shears, saws, hammers, mallets, and hundreds of metal stamps. But I was most intrigued by six notebook pages duct-taped to the wall—geometric compass drawings of exquisite *zellij* tiles like the ones decorating traditional Moroccan buildings all over North Africa. The center of each page was hypnotic, like a candle drawing me to another plane.

"The geometric patterns are ancient," Hamza said. "We see them in Roman art. Islam borrowed them and added new meaning." Hamza talked about sacred geometry—the idea that geometric shapes and proportions can have spiritual meaning. "In all Islamic art there is a center," he said. "The center represents *tawaf*—the Islamic ritual of pilgrimage."

As Hamza talked, I focused on the drawings both in awe and in frustration. I couldn't shake the feeling that there was something deeper here—something I couldn't quite grasp.

◆◆◆

That disconnected feeling was all too familiar—like having thoughts trapped in a swirl of cotton candy. The cause was a stroke I'd suffered years before. Unfortunately, my "sticky thinking" and memory lapses had worsened over the past two years. I sometimes wondered how long I'd be able to travel to places like Fez.

When I'd passed through this medieval walled city on a one-day visit three years earlier, I'd been entranced by its authenticity. The Fez Medina—or Fes el Bali—is a UNESCO World Heritage Site. It's also one of the world's most ancient living cities where some 80,000 people live in a gothic warren of shops, markets, houses, workshops, restaurants, mosques and guesthouses (called *dars* or *riads*). The sometimes-dilapidated buildings are jumbled along 9,000 narrow streets and passageways. It's dense, chaotic, colorful, and alive.

I'd jumped at the chance to return to Fez with this small band of adventurers organized by Deep Travel Workshops. I loved that the program brought us into contact with the medina's artists and allowed time to explore the museums and craft studios. Since I was new to this group, I just hoped

I'd be able to hold my own.

Things did not begin well.

The heart of the Fez Medina is not its center. Viewed on a map, Fes el Bali looks like a blob about a mile west to east and a half–mile north to south. The action spots cluster near the gates at either end and along a northern corridor called the "Big Road," Talaa Kebira. The geographic center is a desert of dusty, labyrinthine streets, keyhole doorways, and dead ends. Our group members were staying in three different guesthouses. Mine, Riad Laayoun, was near the center of the labyrinth.

It wasn't easy for any of us to navigate back and forth to the shopping and craft districts. With my damaged cognition, I planned to stick with my travelmates as often as possible.

After our morning with Hamza, the group scattered for a free afternoon. I returned to Riad Laayoun to drop off my notebooks and grab a jacket. I was surprised to find it deserted. My housemates must have headed straight out after the workshop.

I climbed to my fourth-floor room where the green-and-turquoise *zellij* stars, so like Hamza's drawings, invited praise to heaven. A hand-tooled lantern cast a dim, burnt-orange glow over a glass table and two, wood-carved chairs. The comfy double bed hugged the walls with just enough room for a bedside table and lamp. A breeze caught the lace curtain through the open window. It would be so easy to burrow into this cozy niche for the rest of the day.

Looking at the geometric tiles in my room, I thought again about Hamza's class and wondered: what does it mean to find the center? Does the center represent the perfection to which we aspire? The struggle to be our best selves? Does the center hold our deepest truth?

I didn't have any answers. But I knew that hiding out in my room was not my style. I would venture out and find my own way from the *riad* to the markets near the Blue Gate.

Two blocks from the front door, I was befuddled. Was it left at the wall painting of the pomegranate? Or right? I squinted helplessly at my too-small map.

A young man approached. He was about thirty, well but casually dressed, his hair in shoulder-length in braids. "Good day. May I help you find something? Are you looking for the Big Road?"

"Thanks but I'm OK. I can find it myself." I smiled and turned right. He followed.

"Here, you need to go the other way. I'll show you. I'm not looking for money. No charge."

I started to wave him off, but something shifted inside. I wasn't sure I believed him about the money. But I liked him. And I was lost.

He extended his hand. "I am Ahmed. My family is Berber. We've lived here for many generations."

"Nice to meet you, Ahmed. I'm Anne."

We climbed uphill, crisscrossing a baffling cluster of passageways. As we walked, the streets seemed to come alive. Two little girls played ball with a calico kitten. An old man in a long gray *djellaba* pushed a cart piled high with oranges as big as softballs. A yogurt and pie stall sat next to a shop selling women's ripped jeans in camo patterns. A leather vendor sold handcrafted pouf ottomans the color of Sahara sand.

Around a corner, Ahmed led me to a recessed, white, stone space—a community oven. In a pit a half-story below the street, a muscular, sweating man in a heavy leather apron and a white knit *kufi* (skullcap) swung a wooden dowel, hoisting pans from a fiery oven.

"Here, come closer." When I hesitated, Ahmed laughed. "It's OK. He's my cousin." The baker grinned and held out a metal pan of fresh roasted peanuts. "Go on, try some," Ahmed urged. They were heavenly.

As we left the bakery, Ahmed set the hook. "My family's carpet store is just down the block. Would you like to visit?"

No! I thought. This is where he makes his money. I don't want to be hoodwinked. Then a second thought winged in. I don't mind carpet shops—as my over-rugged house testifies. I grinned. "Sure, we can go—but just to look."

The small shop was like Aladdin's lair, piled floor to ceiling with room-sized carpets, small rugs, and tapestries. Mountain brown, sunset orange, indigo and sky blue... cotton, wool, even camel hair...some woven with geometric forms, others with tribal designs. Ahmed's other "cousin," Hakim, the shop owner, was my guide. Two younger assistants kept the carpets flying. I kept things real by insisting on small rugs only. In the course of half an hour, we flipped through a dozen or so. But nothing wowed me until one of the boys tossed down a bright red carpet, about 28 x 44 inches—the size of a small prayer rug. It was heavy, tightly woven, embroidered with Berber symbols.

Hakim read my expression. "That's an old one. Maybe fifty years. It's camel hair, and natural dye of the mountain poppy. He pulled the rug up onto the bench where we sat. I felt the dense weave and fingered the design. He explained the symbols—the line of life, mountains, protection from the evil eye.

It felt like more than a rug—it felt like a magic carpet to some place I might need to go. Even the price seemed fair.

◆ ◆ ◆

The next morning at Riyad Laayoun, I awoke to the *muezzin's* call to prayer, a rooster's crow, footfalls on *zellij* tiles. It occurred to me that my days of finding my own way might be coming to a close. I took a breath to let that sink in. Was Fez a test? By surrendering to Fez on its own terms, by accepting the help that was offered, by paying the price—

camel hair carpet and all—perhaps I'd touched my own center.

As to the rest of my journey, I have a magic red carpet to help me find the way.

Anne Sigmon won the Suitcase Award for the best essay at the annual Book Passage Travel Writers & Photographers Conference in 2018. Her prize was a Deep Travel Workshop, and she joined our adventure in Morocco.

Photo by Omar Chennafi

Call to Prayer

MARTHA EZELL

I missed the call the third day I was away from it—the call to pay attention, the call to be grateful, the call to be together, the call that unites us.

I'd never visited a Muslim country before. Like many others of my nation, I held a one-dimensional view of a vast and ancient religion practiced more outside than inside our borders. I associated Islam with conflict. I heard reports of women's inferior status within Muslim countries. I naively believed there was little to learn from these places.

Still, I'd traveled enough to realize the importance of experiencing somewhere you don't truly understand, so when the opportunity came to travel to Morocco with a small group of writers, I packed my bags. We'd start in Fez, one of its oldest cities.

From the second floor window of my *riad*, I spot a worker standing in the garden below, away from the central courtyard and behind a row of tall orange trees. He is staring at a rug on the ground with a picture on it: A house? A temple? He is talking to himself. Is he trying to decide whether to buy this rug? It looks almost new. He stares at it for several minutes, and then drops to his knees and puts his head to the ground. Of course, I realize: he is praying. Not for the first time, I feel foolish at my cultural ignorance.

We are invited to dinner at another restored *riad* in the oldest part of Fez. The medina of Fes el Bali is believed to be the largest contiguous pedestrian urban area in the world. We navigate our way through several of the longest and narrowest passageways where I can reach out and touch both walls on each side of me for blocks on end.

As we pass through the markets, I notice there are only men are behind the stalls. They sell multi-colored bins of aromatic spices, hand-sewn clothes, intricate weavings, and an infinite variety of offerings for everyday Moroccan life. They wish me *bonjour* from under their hoods.

However, women are not—as I may have envisioned—out of sight. They are standing in doorways greeting their children as they return home from school, they are out shopping, often arm-in-arm. They visit together while they wait for their bread dough to be cooked in a community oven. They are friendly when asked for directions. Their headscarfs and *djellabas* look comfortable, not "limiting" as I had imagined.

When we at last arrive at the *riad*, we dine in the old mansion's interior courtyard around the customary fountain under a canopy of orange trees. Our hosts are an Australian couple who now raise a family in Fez far past the conventional age when most people become parents.

"We never wanted a family before we came to Fez," they tell us. "The life of Western families always seems to divide the attention of the parents between working and caring for their kids. In Morocco there is not this division. There is a cohesiveness to family life here that Western cultures seem to be missing."

♦♦♦

The next day, a young Moroccan named Zakia leads our group to a courtyard house in Fez. She is anything but shy— a modern version of the Muslim woman, navigating her way boldly though the heavily laden donkeys and pushcarts that deliver all that is needed inside the walled city. She seems comfortable with the time-worn traditions, always with a stylish headscarf, never suggesting she desires a different kind of life. She leads us to the partially vacant house where she was born in the heart of the old medina.

"I want to open a café here and have beautiful dresses like the ones we wear for special occasions available for tourists and visitors to try on and take pictures, along with tea, storytelling, and readings," she tell us. We try on the elaborately embroidered and beaded gowns in intense colors of pink, purple, and deep blue, and take turns taking photos.

She will find her way here just fine, I think, even if not allowed to sell anything in the stalls. This is for her brothers. She seems to have no worry about where she is unable to go. I see how she fits into a larger picture of Muslim life, one that is structured with clear traditions supporting a family-based society. It seems gentle, orderly, nourishing. It is not a perception that I could have understood from a distance. This feels like true Islam.

Zakia leads us the next day to visit the local *hammam*, the communal bathhouse. We enter on the women's side, where mothers are chatting and bathing their young children, sitting together in their underwear in a room full of steam on a tiled floor surely used for hundreds of years.

I lie on the floor as a large attendant in sizable panties rolls me over and covers me from bottom to top with cleansing mud. I'm scrubbed down like an omelet-encrusted pan. There is no modesty within these walls. We are all more alike than different here, and the women nearby, deep in conversation, accept our presence graciously and with little notice.

We walk back out into the narrow byways where the streets have quieted. Friday is the holy day for Islam, and shops close at noon. There is a rush to lock up stores as I hear the call to prayer start, reminding all of their commitment to pray five times each day. The men hurry through the side door of the mosque, slipping off their shoes to go inside. I peek into the doorway to see the rows of men kneeling together, heads to the ground. We are waved away from this entrance. Women enter though a different door to find their community prayers.

Across from the mosque, I find a well-dressed, grey-haired man stooped over a loom in his shop finishing one last weaving. The sheath of material in front of him is a crisscross of delicate fibers of white cotton with bands of agave silk running through it in stripes of bright sea-blue. It is fresh off the loom. I look at it through the light as it draws me in, reflecting the symmetry, the delicate beauty, the patterned calm that exists beneath and alongside the confounding commotion of Fez.

Returning from this brief journey I know that I have only lightly touched the surface of Muslim customs. But as a traveler, I am a visual and kinesthetic learner, and maybe some things can only be understood this way. Tasting complex tagine stews cooked just for me, watching children play ball off narrow walls, hearing joyful women bathe, receiving the unguarded warmth of hooded strangers, opened me up to a culture practiced by almost a fourth of the world's population. I will be back.

I bring the woven material home and send it to my go-to seamstress, my 95-year-old mother who still loves to sew. These curtains created by the elders of two nations now hang in my bedroom window. They filter the morning sunlight, bringing with it a distant understanding, calling me to prayer.

In Deep Travel

ZAKIA ELYOUBI

I am a local
I am a tourist
I am a guide
I am a host
I am a guest
I am a sister
I am a mom
I am a friend
I am a nurse
I am a listener
I am a storyteller
I am a comedian
I am a writer
I am energy
I am love
We are different
We are the same
We are family
We are one

Photo by Tania Amochaev

Do You Remember Me?

TANIA AMOCHAEV

"Hello my friend. Do you remember me?"

I looked up as a donkey jostled the stranger approaching me in the square of the small town. A vague memory flickered, and I felt a smile starting. But my days with the slick touts in the souk of Marrakesh—where I had started this trip to Morocco—had toughened me up.

I had learned through repeated miscalculations that in the souk "Hello, again" is one of the most common tactics used by relentless shopkeepers. An instinctive politeness makes you respond—assuming this is a person you have met. And then you are doomed. Doomed. You are lured into looking at a profusion of pottery, a superfluity of scarves, an alphabet soup of spices, rugs for countless palaces, jewels to adorn harems. *Babouches! Djellabas! Caftans!* A plethora of pastiche in a complex, meandering maze.

Surely I had left this intrusive, intense and relentless pursuit of my dollars behind?

I was spending a few days in the northern hill town of Moulay Idriss, a holy place where Islam was first introduced to Morocco many centuries ago. It felt like a place of calm, beyond the chaos. I was readjusting to people who wanted no more than recognition in return for their welcome.

I stopped and looked more closely at this man. He

returned my gaze expectantly.

Just a few hours earlier I had explored nearby Volubilis, spectacular Roman ruins in the countryside. Ready to head back to my hotel, I was pleased to find a local taxi outside the ruins. The driver waved me toward the back door of the old car. I opened the door, only to wish I hadn't; it was crowded with bodies—male bodies.

Swarthy young men lowered their eyes, then shifted to make room. I jumped in and the taxi lurched off, stopping suddenly as a hand pounded on the window. Space was made for one more passenger who nimbly leaped toward the back, then almost tripped as his eyes met mine.

"Salaam-alaikum," he said, the traditional Arabic greeting meaning "peace be upon you." *"D'où venez vous?"* he added, after righting himself.

We were on a dirt road heading toward town. The guy next to me was muttering on his phone, and—other than furtive glances confirming the unexpected nature of my presence—everyone had pretended to ignore me. They were just as surprised to be joined by a foreigner the age of their grandmothers as I had been to realize the taxi was a shared one.

"De Californie," I replied.

"Ah," he continued, *"et que pensez vous du Maroc?"*

What did I think of Morocco? All eyes fastened onto me, even the driver's, in the rearview mirror.

"Je l'aime beaucoup! Les gens sont très gentilles!" I answered, confirming my love for his country and the kindness of its people.

"Merci, merci," he thanked me, before translating my reply for the others. Tensions eased, and Mohammed—as he introduced himself—switched from French to the more challenging English. He worked as a history teacher in a neighboring village.

We pulled over for yet another passenger whose *"Salaam"*

stretched and faded into *"alaaaiiikum..."* as he stared at me. When he smiled, I offered my hand. Soon everyone was shaking it, some forgetting to let go. Men holding an unknown woman's hand was clearly something unusual here.

"This was Morocco's first city," Mohammed started. But before going any further, he shouted an urgent "Stop!" and jumped out. He bowed to me before parting, tossing a coin to the driver. I got out soon after.

Now, some hours later, I did remember him.

"Of course! So good to see you again."

He smiled and nodded, continuing on his way after wishing me a good visit.

Still warmed by the unexpected encounter with Mohammed, I continued my walk around town. I passed the street stand where I had eaten tagine with friends the night before. The chef, Abdo, had uncovered several gorgeous peaks of vegetables artistically layered in now-familiar clay dishes with conical tops—they, too, called tagines. After, he insisted I pose with him for a photo.

Further on, I met a young woman herding some children along a blue alley.

"C'est Fatima," she said with a laugh, indicating the daughter now hanging onto my hand as if it were a rare gift. *"Et je m'appelle Zora."*

"Ce n'est pas possible!" I exclaimed.

I am not sure the woman understood when I explained she shared my mother's name; but, once I taught her five-year-old son to use my phone, we huddled for a family portrait—with the American.

When I stopped to take a picture of a donkey munching some greens in the countryside, a young lad jumped on its back and stood up to make the picture more interesting. When I sat on a cement ledge next to a mosque, a shoe shiner handed me a seat cushion, warming my heart almost as much as my bottom. Later, when I passed a girl in a doorway and blew her a kiss, her mother gaily shouted "*bisou!*" She then brought another infant barreling from behind the door and into my arms. We laughed as we spun in circles.

On my arrival a day earlier, I had approached Moulay Idriss alone and on foot. It was my second visit, so I wasn't worried about getting lost. As I walked, a group of young men materialized around me, slowing to match my pace. I slowed further. So did they.

Was I mad to be out here alone?

Any momentary concerns were immediately allayed as, rather than to an attack, I fell victim to their persistent charm. One of the men spoke French, another some English. They serenaded me, accompanied by metal double castanets—called a *qraqeb*—which they tried to teach me to play. We walked and sang, the leader calling out the key word, the rest of us intoning in response. I had no idea what we were singing, but there was joy and laughter and music. Time flew.

Eventually we passed four young women who slowed and stared at me. I paused, worried that the guys were singing something embarrassing; that they were perhaps laughing *at* me, rather than *with* me. But a girl who understood my French confirmed they were, indeed, singing very nicely. The two groups smiled at each other, tentatively.

When we moved on, I learned that earlier the men had been snubbed by the same group of women. The girls were Berber, the boys Arab. They suspected this as the cause, although one explained that his mother, too, was Berber. Now that they had a rather unusual chaperone, a door seemed to have opened. I was thrilled that my presence could help the two groups to open up to each other.

We approached town, posing for photos for one last time before parting. Idriss, who studied informatics, asked me to send him a group picture. I noted his email address, then shook hands with each one of the young men, knowing they were reluctant to let me go.

"*Tu es la première Américaine que j'ai jamais touchée,*" the last one said, clasping my arm. Perhaps he had dreamed that the first American woman he touched would be a seductive beauty, someone more akin to who he might have encountered if he had met me many years earlier. All the same, the young Moroccan looked me in the eye and smiled warmly, touching me that much more deeply.

◆ ◆ ◆

All too soon, my trip was over.

Back in America, the news poured out in a relentless flood, the media hawking their points of view like touts in a global souk. A brute in the White House. Rising global tensions. The radical Islam of ISIS. Hatred and horror, anger and fear.

I sit here now, taking a break from the ugliness, looking at photographs from my trip. A town on a hill glows in otherworldly light. A kid standing on a donkey grins. The beauty of vegetable tagines complements Abdo's smile. Zora leans close while her children fuss. And eight, slightly scruffy youths look both shy and protective at the same time.

I might not recognize these young men if I encountered them again on the street, just as at first I hadn't recognized Mohammed. But I was now Facebook friends with Abdo and Idriss, so I posted pictures and video of our encounters. I loved seeing the comments from their friends and mine. One translated as "Gratitude from the official sponsor of tourism for Moulay Idriss": بمولاي للسياحة الرسمي الراعي كبور زرمون ادريس. Others marveled at what their world looked like through my eyes.

In response to my post of our songfest, Idriss wrote, "I

will never forget this moment." As tears I don't even try to hold back attest, neither will I.

Yes, my friends, I certainly do remember you.

I do remember you.

Tania Amochaev and friends

The Fez Medina rooftops
Photo by Christina Ammon

Morocco, Home, and Heaven

LIBBY CHANEY

Chickens caught in a small wooden cage, climbing over each other, flapping, squawking. They are screaming, really. As the butcher watches us walk by, he's blithely pulling the guts from a carcass. He's easily within earshot of the chickens in the cage.

I love chicken tagine with lemon and olives. I cannot hear the chicken scream.

I don't feel the hands of the chicken gutter on my guts.

I hear two men arguing in Arabic, their language like a shaking bag of rocks. And then a laugh and slaps on the sleeves of wool. And they walk in opposite directions, still laughing.

I smell peas cooking on a tiny clay chimney in a pie tin. Three men sit down around the little red fire for the little green peas, smiling, smiling, smiling.

The seller selling honey cookies relaxes in his stall with the bees. Bees are doing research on the cookies. We all know full well why.

I like preserved lemons: the color, the taste of sunlight— bitter, soft and soaked with juice and olives with their oil.

I like to brush my teeth without wondering if the water's safe. When that faucet's water's in my mouth alone, like a river I am swimming in, I wonder if I'll die from it, or just get a little sick, or if my minty toothpaste is discouragement enough for germs.

I slowly put one old foot over one damaged knee, going up, already worried about coming down. Blue and white tile patterns on the stairs—a distraction from my grief.

Back home on a sunny deck in Cleveland now, the air would be too cold to enjoy the wind. I could tell myself to stay in Fez, except for the bulbs pushing up by my door.

Afternoon walking in the medina from light into darkness and back again. The walls are sometimes blue, then pink along the way, but from above they look like sand.

Our dog Raisa would love the call to worship. Five times a day she would sing along, reminding us to contact our creator.

I love the slightly open door, and I am not afraid to look inside, like the sight of lace inside a woman's blouse.

"I want to taste your money" the seller murmurs—he is so romantic!

"What's your best price?" another demands, blocking our exit from his shop.

You get lots of knots in burl wood; it grows under earth above the roots, below the stem.

You can choose loblolly pine or the lemon, too, for different reasons. All good.

Farmers arrange piles of carrots next to herbs in our farmers' markets, like here in the souk. We eat the same food, preparing differently.

And we have doors and windows, but none like these. Not in Home Depot, anyway.

These doors let you know you're entering something other than a place and show you what shape you are. I think they point toward heaven.

I see some people with tragic feet wearing plastic slippers on the street. One ankle turned like a burl. One foot turned toward the sky, but walking.

Three little boys. It's late at night, sitting on a doorstep in the market, laughing, laughing, laughing.

Donkeys loaded with our heavy bags of pleasant clothes and toothbrushes choose their way up the stairs.

Back home, Donna's disease had come with a visa for either heaven or for hell. She visited hell for a while at the doctors. When her children came, she took the first flight out. Through a window in a gown, I think. She sent me a message in my dream, in the midst of my own, much smaller adventure in Fez. "Arrived safely!" she said.

This vignette appeared on the *Deep Travelogue* blog.

Photo by Christina Ammon

The Whole Desert is a Living Souk

FERNANDO MANRIQUE

Slowly, and without the usual politeness of saying good night, one person at a time stood from the cushions around the camp dinner table and left the fading campfire. Each disappeared into the cool shadows of the all-embracing desert night beyond.

Maybe they felt lured by the silence of the endless dunes of the Moroccan Sahara at nighttime. Or perhaps they needed privacy to contemplate the vastness of the sky which opened like a dark umbrella of infinite stars competing for attention. Or perhaps it was to digest the delicious Berber *couscous* we just had for dinner. Or maybe a plain need for rest. Who knows?

The last shadow of those wandering away disappeared, leaving just three of us guests behind. Ali and Kich, our two Berber guides, started to clear the dinner table, and we quietly helped them, all of us unconsciously doing our best to sustain the momentum of desert silence. We then rearranged the cushions around the fading fire. We grew still and faced the flames, wrapped in the warmth of our camel wool under the blinking stars.

Allowing myself to indulge in the different body

sensations of tiredness and post-dinner relaxation, and with my soul contently floating in the stillness of the desert night, my mind started to unfold the experiences of the day. I reflected on my childhood fantasies of the desert.

I grew up watching movie dramas set in exotic locales around the world and afterwards play-acted being a South Sea pirate, a Western cowboy, an Indian prince, a Crusader or Saladin, and above all, Laurence of Arabia. What a life full of adventure and danger Laurence (and me!) did have— wearing white clothes, riding an Arabian stallion from one caravanserai to another through the Jordan, the Nefud, and Sinai desert. We'd find food and forage while raiding the Ottomans during WWI.

So, when my friend Christina invited me to join her organized spiritual traveling group heading to the Moroccan Sahara, how could I say no and skip this opportunity to ride through a real desert and replay some childhood adventures?

Early that morning, we left on jeeps from an outpost near the last Berber village at the foot of *Erg Chebbi*, a 22-kilometer long dune and a respectable herald of the Moroccan Sahara. We were heading to a "meeting point" from where we would start our caravan for a two-day desert trip. I was very excited by the prospect that our starting point would be the ideal one of any desert travel: a caravanserai!

Caravanserais were trading posts composed of a *kasbah* (fortress) or the circled tents of nomad people next to an oasis or a desert well. They lay seemingly scattered at random, like beads of a broken necklace across a yellow blanket of sand, but were connected through invisible threads only evident for the nomads. Caravanserais shine under the relentless sun, like coins dropped in the sand. People within these dynamic microcosms shout in incomprehensible languages, trade and bargain goods, services, sweet-tasting dates, and exotic-smelling food. The places are also filled with the loud growls of grumpy camels, the whinnies of sweaty horses, and the happy screams of kids playing around, indifferent to the oppressive heat. Nowhere but here are you able to sense the flow of invisible feelings of arriving travelers: the ones tired but happy to end their trip and the ones anxious to depart. All dwell in tents cooling, resting, and refreshing themselves before a next move.

Well, our "meeting point" did not resemble my dreamed caravanserai at all: it was a dried bush standing alone in the middle of nowhere about half a mile away from the tiny village nearby. Slowly, however, our caravan did start to be form after the jeep drivers loudly phoned Ali and Kech to come meet us. While we waited, Omar, a teenager, appeared from the village on a shabby old motorbike wearing a trendy T-shirt and tight jeans and listening to music through the headsets of his mobile phone.

A few minutes later, two kids appeared on their bikes bringing the first camels: eight little toy souvenir dromedaries crafted from straw and colorful fabric. These young Berber entrepreneurs keenly offered them in broken French and English. Meanwhile, we travelers stood awkwardly outside the jeeps next to our dead bush trying to figure out what was happening and what to do. We posed our many questions to the drivers, but they did not speak English.

I then spotted our guides in the distance bringing the real camels. As they approached, it struck me how similarly the animals and their guides moved: all walked with a calm, long, and pendular cadence, possibly conditioned by a lifestyle without a need for time-keeping, or by the speed-breaking heat of inclement sunshine.

Our caravanserai also kept transforming. Most of my white-skinned travel companions, unaccustomed to the rising temperature, silently clustered in a small shadow made by the jeep, like king penguins utterly lost in the desert. They sipped from water bottles, seeking protection and relief from the overwhelming heat. The spiritual leader of the group wandered like a lost butterfly, smelling and munching some dried, lonely fruit from a forgotten single bush in the endless life-challenging landscape. The young guide, Omar, metamorphosed himself from a modern global silent teenager and became our third Berber guide wearing a turban, a blue *djellaba,* and an inscrutable Berber expression.

As the guides arrived with the animals, my hope of riding a horse like Laurence quickly died. They brought only camels. Still, my curiosity of riding such a desert being for a longer time than at the tourist parks in Marrakesh did not leave any space for disappointment. Luckily our older guides, the deep-voiced Ali and the always-smiling Kech spoke English, so the preliminary greetings and introductions were swiftly made, and they immediately assigned a camel to each of us.

My companions and the camels exchanged incredulous gazes, measuring each other with mistrust and awe. Mine was definitely not a stallion and kept dribbling and grumbling all the time, especially at the moment of standing up and sitting down. Sitting on a camel while it stands up or lies down is like being on rollercoaster inside a blender—a highly recommended experience for those who want to mix all seven directions at the same time and lose and regain orientation in three seconds!

And, at last, we started our journey. The camel ride to our next camp followed a well-worn track. This part did resemble my fantasies—at least the shadow rows of camels slowly pacing from one dune crest to the next. Unexpectedly, we heard the loud engine sounds of four-wheel drive jeeps and quads passing our slow caravan out of sight behind nearby dunes. I felt I was driving in the slowest lane of a sandy highway to a faraway point I would never reach on my camel.

After barely an hour riding, we reached our camp, a

raised salt flat partially surrounded by *ergs*, or sand dunes. Again, no date palms, no oasis, no nomads living in colorful tents to be seen, but instead, four, well-delineated camps of other travel companies complete with other young travelers. Some were discovering the modern joy of sand-boarding on the closest dune.

◆ ◆ ◆

Coming back to the reality of the present moment there at the fading fire under that infinite spread of stars, I became aware that so far, only a few of my childhood reminiscences had come true. Aside from dressing myself that morning in white clothes and a green turban and pretending to be a non-belligerent 21st-century Laurence of Morocco, and aside from the excitement of riding a real camel in a real desert for the first time, nothing else remained.

The historical Laurence of Arabia once said: "The abstraction of the desert landscape cleansed me." As a regular meditator for years, I could relate to his desire for inner cleansing. My impulse to join this spiritual travel group and to meditate in the desert aligned with Laurence's view of the desert as a vast, healing temple of nature.

Well, after arriving at our camp late that afternoon, I was determined to meditate in the desert and absorb its cleansing and healing powers. For that purpose, I decided to take a walk as far as I could without getting lost and find an ideal spot of silence and solitude for my meditative practice.

On my way to find a secluded spot, I passed patches of desert bushes. Among and around them, I found many tracks of running shoes, motorbikes, and jeeps, as well as empty bottles of water, candy wrappers, used toilette paper, and even condoms. Apparently, many people were using the desert as a cleansing spot for many things.

Looking for a perfect spot, I continued my walk for half

an hour until finally, I found a track-free place where three little dunes converged around a lonely small bush. Full of gratitude to the Universe for bringing me to this ideal place, I assumed my usual sitting posture with crossed legs, open eyes and inhaling through a slightly open mouth—ready for my first meditation experience in the stillness of the desert.

However, the Universe had other plans. From the very instant I sat down, I was constantly challenged by big desert flies arriving from nowhere. Keen explorers of my nostrils and open eyes, they were particularly persistent in kissing me in the lips—even slipping into my mouth. These flying sentient beings were trying to show me the path of inward journey to the true self. Closing my eyes and mouth didn't seem to help much in gaining the needed calmness to meditate. Making matters worse, the sunset seemed to bring more flies toward me, and the ensuing cold triggered goosebumps on my skin. I sat in my Laurence-like, white-linen clothes feeling tense.

This was not the first time I had attempted to meditate in the company of insects; however, their number and intensity were just too much for a simple, average practitioner like me.

So I gave up.

Bowing to the desert in gratitude for the experience, I started walking back to the camp—not with a feeling of defeat but more with the insight that fantasies and preformed ideas might not match with the reality of the physical world.

Still, lying on the cushion in front of the dying fire, I became aware that everyone had left to their tents. The day felt like a dream. As I finally succumbed to the forces of sleep, the events of the day passed again through my mind like sand falling inside an hourglass. I realized something Laurence didn't: the whole desert is a living souk!

Souvenir

ALICIA ANDRAE

I hold in my hands a cheap, red-and-white-striped nylon bag, bought on impulse in the Fez Medina. I'd spotted it hanging from the ceiling in a shop while searching for gifts to give friends and family back home. I wandered the twisting labyrinth of the markets on my quest, breathing in dusty air that smelled of spice, citrus, and leather. Scent highlights changed as I moved from souk to souk, (the smell of chicken poop and rotting flesh dominated the meat market), but baseline notes were always the same: dust and spice, citrus and leather.

This bag is huge. The material is thin and feels almost papery, but at least it has a zipper. It will have a single purpose: to be a repository and transit vessel for goods headed from one continent to another. Early tomorrow, as solemn echoes of the morning's call to prayer still hover in the sky, I will fill it with treasures from this place:

- One pair of pointy-toed, florally embossed, peacock-blue *babouches*, size six. My first experience haggling in the street. I overpaid.
- Six handbags, three scarves, and a table runner. A rainbow of textiles made on ancient looms by men with few teeth. I have pictures.

- Twelve tiny ceramic tagines (blue and white), two soap dishes, one mug, and four serving platters of various sizes (also blue and white), acquired in a shop where I broke the first thing I touched. The shopkeeper wouldn't let me pay for it.
- Four ancient trilobite fossils, wrenched from the earth by a Berber man with a donkey. "Special price," just for me.
- Two embellished square hand drums and one stringed instrument whose name I cannot recall, bought in the back room of an eclectic music shop where traditional *ouds* share wall space with violins. I got a free music lesson with purchase. And,
- One hammered brass bangle bracelet, imprinted with never ending vines. A gift from an unexpected friend.

I'll cocoon it all in cellophane and packing tape so that the bag doesn't split apart at the seams in transit: from Fez to Lisbon, from Lisbon to Madrid, and finally from Madrid, home.

After a good night's sleep, I'll slice open this unwieldy, otherworldly fruit, spilling its bounty onto my suburban American floor. As friends and family *ooh* and *ahh* over their gifts, comparing this to that, trading one scarf for another, laughing as they try to play the handmade instruments, the sounds of their voices will remind me that one of the treasures of travel is returning home. When I collect the now-empty bag, destined for the recycling bin, I will lift it up, hold it to my heart.

I will inhale one last breath of Fez Medina air.

Dust and spice, citrus and leather.

Contributors

On the roof of Riad Zany in Fez, Morocco with Tim Cahill, 2017

CHRISTINA AMMON has penned stories on a wide range of topics, from flying with raptors in Nepal to exploring the underground wine scene in Morocco. She received the Oregon Literary Arts Fellowship for creative nonfiction, and her travel writing and photos have appeared in *BBC, Condé Nast, Hemispheres,* the *San Francisco Chronicle,* the *Los Angeles Times, The Oregonian,* and many other publications.

She is the founder of Deep Travel Workshops. **DeepTravelWorkshops.com**

TANIA ROMANOV AMOCHAEV is an avid traveler, writer, and photographer. She has climbed Mount Whitney and Mount Kenya, circumnavigated Annapurna, trekked Bhutan and Kashmir, and sailed rivers in Burma and India. She traveled Russia during the years of Communism, walked across Kenya during the 2013 terrorist attacks, and traveled Bangladesh during that country's 2018 elections. Tania was born in Belgrade, Serbia of two displaced émigrés—a White Russian father and a Croatian mother—and spent her childhood in a refugee camp. In her book, *Mother Tongue: A Saga of Three Generations of Balkan Women*, she explores, in a highly personal saga, the Balkan struggles over the last hundred years. **www.TaniaAmochaev.com**

ALICIA ANDRAE is a writer and traveler whose diverse loves of family, food, books, nature, and human connections have led her to a Turkish restaurant in Paris, into Australia's Red Centre on camelback, and traipsing through the South African bush in search of mopane worms, stick insects, and dung beetles. Her past lives have included stints as a corporate lawyer, second-grade teacher, and swim instructor. She can be found online at **RoamingFromHome.com**.

SIOBHANN BELLINGER is a San Francisco born and based travelista who lives to explore the new. Some of her preferred photography subjects are snacks, cityscapes, graffiti and street cats. She recently bought a right-hand drive Japanese van and is documenting her road warrior adventures in Northern California and beyond. Her travel photography and musings can be found online at **DetourDelights.com** and she posts as @detourdelights on many a social platform.

MIKE BERNHARDT is an award-winning writer whose stories have been published by *Hidden Compass* and *Journey Beyond Travel.* He edited and contributed to an anthology of poetry about grief called *Voices of the Grieving Heart,* and his poetry also appeared in *Finding What You Didn't Lose* by John Fox. When he's not writing or traveling, Mike cooks Thai food, plays Caribbean steel drums, and enjoys the outdoors. He lives in the San Francisco Bay Area with his wife Yvonne, their two cats, and their son when he's not away at college. You can read more about Mike's travels on his blog: **TravelingWithMikeAndYvonne.com.**

MARIA BITARELLO is a Brazilian writer, translator, and journalist brought up between her home country and the United States. With a masters degree in Luso-Brazilian Literature from UCLA, she has worked as a book editor; a film-, music-, and theater producer; a newspaper reporter; and has taught English and Portuguese abroad. She's also a Sagittarius and a member of the theater company Teatro Oficina, in São Paulo (Brazil), where she has been based since 2012. She's the author of two creative non-fiction books, both published in Brazil: *Só sei que foi assim* (La Petite Ferme, 2014 & 2018) and *O tempo das coisas* (In Medias Res, 2018), and had a short story published in the American anthology *Vignettes & Postcards from Paris* (Reputation Books, 2012), in addition to a number of pieces on Brazilian magazines and websites. Her blog is **IOnceMetAGirl.com**.

LISA BOICE: When not working her corporate job as a communications manager, Lisa Boice and her husband travel the world in search of birds (though she doesn't tell her mother that she's looking for birds like the bushtit, cock-of-the-rock, and booby). Lisa is a recipient of a Bronze Solas Award, and she blogs at **TheAccidentalBirder.com.**

STACY BOYINGTON is a native Californian, residing in Marin County. She is a seeker of beauty in writing, art, home, food, and travel. Stacy writes memoir essays and travel non-fiction. Life adventures include owning a Mexican restaurant, driving a vintage convertible, directing a fine art gallery, living on a boat, and attempting to learn French. She also loves riding horses, Nordic skiing, walking fast, and tacos. Her love of simple pleasures and spending time with her grown children and grandson are her compass.

Deep Travel dines in Marrakesh with Erin Byrne, 2015
Photo by Anna Elkins

ERIN BYRNE is the author of *Wings: Gifts of Art, Life, and Travel in France,* editor of *Vignettes & Postcards from*

Paris and *Vignettes & Postcards from Morocco,* and writer of *The Storykeeper* film. Erin's work has won Grand Prize Solas Awards for Travel Story of the Year, the Foreword Indies Book of the Year, an Accolade Award for film, and the Pinnacle Achievement Award. She has taught writing at Shakespeare & Company in Paris, at Book Passage, and on Deep Travel trips, and is host of the LitWings event series at Book Passage and in Paris which features writers, photographers, and filmmakers. Erin is Collaborating Curator of Travel Writing and Photography for The Creative Process Exhibition, which travels to the world's leading universities. Her screenplay, *Siesta,* is in pre-production in Spain, and she is working on a novel set in the Paris Ritz during the occupation, *Illuminations.* **E-Byrne.com**

LIBBY CHANEY is an artist. She was born, raised, and educated in Ohio. In the 1960s, when she was in her twenties, she wandered off to California, where she inadvertently lived for 47 years. She taught there, traveled a bit, married, and had two children. After her son suddenly died, she was drawn back to her Ohio at Lake Erie. She now lives in a sunlit studio, able to work as an artist every single day with her third and final husband, Paul Waszink, and a cat named Charles. **LibbyChaney.com**

OMAR CHENNAFI lives in Fez, Morocco where he is a photographer for the Ministry of Tourism and where he has been an official photographer for The Sacred Music Festival. His photos have appeared in many publications, including *TIME* magazine. Chennafi's work mediates two perspectives: that of the tourists who treasure the Fez Medina as a UNESCO World Heritage Site and the perspective of residents who often view it as a forgotten heritage. Chennafi seeks to bridge these two worlds with his images.

DICK DALTON, co-Creator at Value Life Associates, is 74 years into his Quest. His collage includes 35 years teaching 20,000 HBCU students as a PhD Health Educator and Life Coach. Other hats he wears or has worn include husband, father, actor, minister, singer/songwriter, Social Artist, playwright, philosopher, editor, hitch-hiker, hospital corpsman, war resister/peace advocate, and author of *I Am NOT My Thoughts*. He can be found on Facebook (Value Life Associates) or on Instagram @daltondster.

MARSHA DALTON is retired from teaching and computer technology. She lives in a small city in Missouri with her husband and four lovely creatures who have plenty of "cattitude." In retired life, Marsha's hobbies are songwriting, reading, traveling, and appreciating the life she has been allowed to live thus far. She looks forward to more time to spend with friends and family. You can find her songs, including "Donkey Day," on **YouTube.com.**

TIM DAW is a photographer originally from Liverpool, England. He has photographed in Morocco, Mexico, and much of Europe and captured political personalities such as Nancy Pelosi, Tom Ammiano, and Barbara Boxer. But Tim's true love is photographing weddings. "I love getting to be with people on the best day of their lives," he says. He now makes his home in Oakland, California.

ANN DUFAUX, a dual citizen, (though claiming to be a citizen of the world), taught many years at Université de Franche Comté in Besançon, France. The mother of four, Ann previously found little time to write except for occasional long letters to friends and relatives. She's presently interested in writing fiction and travel pieces, and after exploring haiku is looking into poetry inspired by personal experience. She has been longlisted two consecutive years for travel stories in Ireland's Fish Publishing competitions. She loves discovering new places and people and has been to Vietnam, India, Greece, Romania, Spain, North Africa, Mexico, and Nicaragua, traveling for work and pleasure. She tries to assimilate language basics in the countries she visits, eager to make friends wherever she goes. She and Jacques, her husband, have hiked the 2,000-kilometer Camino Frances to Compostela and are pursuing other trails two weeks a year. She loves nature, reading, singing, and practicing Tai Chi.

ANNA ELKINS is a traveling poet and painter. She earned a BA in English & art and an MFA and Fulbright Fellowship in poetry. Anna has written, painted, and taught on six continents, publishing her writing and exhibiting her art along the way. She has won some things and lost many others. She has illustrated several books and authored four of her own, including the poetry collection *The Space Between.* Anna helps lead Deep Travel Workshops and also teaches classes that play in the crossroads of art + word + spirit, both near her home in Oregon and far, far away. **AnnaElkins.com**

ZAKIA ELYOUBI was born and raised in Fez. She studied English literature and has taught English at a local language center. With several friends, she started an association called "Friends of Fez Orphans" that helps abandoned children in Fez. Zakia has always loved listening to stories, and that love inspired her to become a storyteller herself. She has been a professional storyteller for six years and is now in the process of developing the Cultural Café, where she celebrates Moroccan culture and the rebirth of the art of storytelling. Her motto is "spread love."

MARTHA EZELL has been writing for a decade from her home just north of San Francisco in Petaluma, California.

After careers in social work, documentary filmmaking, and educational technology, she has left the daily workforce to pursue her love of travel, writing, art, and the outdoors. Her writing has been published in *The Best Women's Travel Writing, Vol. 8, Gadling,* and on the *Deep Travelogue* blog.

Deep Travel in Fez with Dot Fisher-Smith 2015

DOT FISHER-SMITH considers herself a Primitive: a hunter-gatherer, minimalist, autodidact—highly relational and process-oriented. She thrives on intimate relationships and loves to backpack alone in the wilderness. She is fascinated by observing the dance of opposites in nature and in herself, the tension between being a householder and her love of the outdoors, between the sedentary tasks she loves (reading, journaling, making art) and her love of hiking, biking, dancing, and swimming. Dot is passionately engaged with the urgency of this very moment. And mountains. She loves connecting people, encouraging and inspiring them— even daring them to push their uniqueness to the max. Her mission is to model that daring.

BONNIE J. FLADUNG specializes in adventure travel writing with a focus on nature and wildlife. She combines her love of literature with a passion for traveling to remote places, and has studied the art of storytelling with master storytellers in Morocco and the San Bushmen of the Kalahari Desert. She is the co-author of the award-winning *When Eagles Roar: The Amazing Journey of an African Wildlife Adventurer,* which was selected as "One of the Best Wildlife Books of All Time" by BookAuthority and is a 2016 National Geographic book recommendation. *The Elephant's Euphonium: A Little Tusker's Adventures in Africa* is her first book in a series of illustrated picture books about overlooked and endangered species that teaches children the importance of conservation. **BonnieFladung.com**

ABBY FRINK: Born sometime before the turn of the last century, Abby Frink can trace her ancestry back to her mother and her father. Here, however, the genealogical trail grows cold, though it is rumored that her ancestors might have been gypsies. Abby excelled at mime kazoo, licking postage stamps, and sewing silk wings for lonesome moles at a very early age. From these disparate skills, a sturdy foundation was laid for her passions of hospice and creative writing. Abby is a nurse, scientist, gardener, cowgirl, and she thinks sheep are ugly. During her spare time, she reads a lot of books, watches reruns of *Antique Roadshow* with her dog Roxi, and travels to Yelapa, Mexico to teach local women to sew cute, stuffed, felt animals. South of the border she is affectionately known simply as Anita.

LARRY HABEGGER is a writer and editor who has been covering the world since his international travels began in the 1970s. As a freelance writer for more than three decades, his work has appeared in many major newspapers and magazines, including the *Los Angeles Times, Chicago Tribune, Travel & Leisure,* and *Outside.* He coauthored serialized mysteries with James O'Reilly for the *San Francisco Examiner* in the early 1980s, and in 1993 he cofounded the award-winning Travelers' Tales publishing company with James and Tim O'Reilly. He is currently Travelers' Tales' executive editor, helps oversee the company's publishing program, and has worked on all of its 150-plus books. Larry teaches the craft of memoir and the personal essay and runs several writers groups. He is also a cofounder of The Prose Doctors—an editors consortium—and editor of the annual magazine *The Travel Guide to California.* He lives with his family on Telegraph Hill in San Francisco.

LarryHabegger.com

Riding donkeys to Moulay Idriss with Larry Habegger, 2018
Photo by Anna Elkins

RUBY TOOTSIE HANES is a pseudonym for Marilyn

Antoinette Hanes. She is a self-made, sovereign woman who lives in Oregon under the gaze of heavenly hosts who have guarded her through tough times and ridiculous situations. She's been in writing groups forever, and this is her first publication. She earned her Associates degree from Orange Coast College in 1979.

STEFANIE HOFFMAN is a writer and mental health activist. Her writing on mental illness has appeared in various publications, including KQED, *Elephant Journal* and *The NAMI Advocate*. She writes the blog *Anything But That: Parenting the Mentally Ill Child* and is currently writing her first book, a memoir, about navigating her daughter's mental health condition. In a prior life, Stefanie was the lead cybersecurity editor and reporter for global tech media publication CRN, where she regularly traveled around the world to interview executives at multinational security companies and write about the latest cyber threats and data breaches. She is a member of the board of directors for the San Francisco chapter of National Alliance on Mental Illness (NAMI). As part of her advocacy efforts, she has given nationally syndicated presentations on childhood mental illness. She also speaks in high schools on how to identify mental illness in youth and teaches a class to parents of children with a mental health condition on how to navigate all aspects of their child's illness.

LAURA HUGHES loves nothing more than to be in the world, exploring new places and cultures, and she is perennially torn about where to settle herself for the next while. She's happiest when traveling somewhere sunny, connecting with people (familiar and new) of all walks of life, engaging in conversation, listening to something great, trying new foods, cooking, mountain biking, and enjoying the outdoors. She also loves dancing salsa and practicing her Spanish. Her career has centered on her passions for food, travel, and people, and among other things (including cooking at Hell's Backbone Grill, a James Beard nominated restaurant in Utah), she worked on food strategy for Starbucks, ran customer service for an international airline, and helped lead two startups. She's currently a leadership coach. She enjoys writing but struggles to persuade herself to be alone for long enough to finish anything! She contributed to Hell's Backbone Grill's cookbook, *This Immeasurable Place: Food and Farming from the Edge of Wilderness.*

NANCY KESSLER made a career in journalism as a writer, editor, and photographer, interspersed with a long list of diverse and unconnected jobs. A former staff member at Time Inc., she has been published in *Time, People, Playboy, The New York Times,* and regional magazines, and she is a former staff member at several newspapers in the Rocky Mountains. She also worked for environmental organizations, arts and cultural centers, an architect, search and rescue, a hospital, saloons, a senior center, in elementary school and university programs, on public policy conferences, and as a dog washer. A native of Chicago, she has resided in New York, London, Wyoming, California, and Montana, where she now lives a few blocks from the Yellowstone River.

KYLE KEYSER is the son of a National Security Agency spy who moved continents every three to five years; so naturally, he became a world traveler who is horrible at keeping secrets (see: "Exploring the Edge: Moroccan Confessionals"). At age 27, he discovered a documentary filmmaking talent when he pretended to be a film director in order to meet his favorite rock star. Political by nature, he became a "citizen advocate" candidate for Atlanta mayor in 2009 where he, fortuitously, did not come in last. Now, Kyle has combined filmmaking with politics and is currently producing creative campaign content for blue-sided candidates in Georgia. He sees a future as a travel writer. For your reference: **Kyle.tv** and **RRatedCreative.com.**

HUDSON LINDENBERGER believes that life is full of interesting stories, and his goal is to tell as many of them as possible. As a full-time freelance writer, he is always searching out and following interesting paths while maintaining a smile on his face. The Boulder, Colorado resident is the father of two adult daughters, an active outdoorsman, avid traveler, and has an unbridled passion for a perfectly concocted cocktail or beer. He recently returned to the United States after living in Lyon, France for two years where he immersed himself in European culture while crisscrossing the continent. It was during this time that he decided to join Deep Travel on a trip to Morocco.

KIMBERLEY LOVATO is a freelance travel journalist and champagne-loving Francophile whose work has appeared in *National Geographic Traveler, AFAR, Virtuoso Life, Private Clubs,* the *San Francisco Chronicle, Delta Sky Magazine, American Way, Robb Report, BBC.com,* and many more prestigious publications. Her personal essays have appeared in several anthologies, including *The Best Women's Travel Writing.* Kimberley is the author of four travel-themed books including her first, *Walnut Wine & Truffle Groves,* which won the SATW Gold Award for book of the year in 2012. Her most recent book, *100 Things To Do In San Francisco Before You Die,* was released by Reedy Press in 2018. **KimberleyLovato.com**

FERNANDO MANRIQUE was born in Peru and traveled during his childhood and youth in several South American countries. Later, he studied medicine around the world, specializing in psychiatry and psychotherapy, public health, and applied ethics. Also following a personal quest, he trained in different spiritual traditions in Hawaii and Peru, and he practices Vajrajana Buddhism with pilgrimages to Japan and Bhutan, among other places. He published a collection of articles about the history of Tantra and translated into German a book about the educational reform of Bhutan. Currently, he lives between Morocco and Switzerland, working as a psychiatrist/psychotherapist, facilitating workshops, and teaching different healing approaches in Europe and Mexico. In Morocco, he aims to develop holistic health promotion programs and to promote the dialogue of people, cultures and spiritual paths in the region. He says: "The world is my home, I just move between rooms."

MOLLY MCKISSICK is a teacher and mother of four grown children. She lives in Ashland, Oregon where she enjoys hiking with her two black dogs, swimming, skiing, and playing the Irish harp. Her passions are working with children and traveling. She has taught kindergarten through eighth grade, and most recently she worked with Rohingya refugee children in Bangladesh. She made a short documentary film of her experience there to help raise awareness about the plight of their endangered culture. The film, *We Are Blood,* is currently screening at festivals world-wide and will soon be available on the Web under that title. Molly wrote her poem, "Far, Far Away" for her fifth graders, and they performed it—with movement—at a school assembly.

TREE KNOWLTON is a clinical herbalist, maker of things, urban homesteader and hooligan. Her partner, children, and grandchildren are generous contributors to her joy...and if

Dreamer the wonder dog could read, she'd probably appreciate being included here too. Tree toils daily with the question, "Am I making good use of my gifts and my privilege?" as our society and politics bob around—nay, flail—in stormy waters.

KEIKO MORIYAMA, an avid traveler, retired from an uneventful career in software marketing and plunged into the world of travel writing. While attending a travel writers' conference at Book Passage (Corte Madera, California), she noticed a stack of flyers promoting a week-long writing workshop in Morocco led by Tim Cahill. "Why not?" she thought and impulsively signed up for the trip. Immersed in the cultural richness of Morocco, Keiko learned the fundamentals of colorful storytelling, how to survive a *hammam* bath, and how not to get desperately lost in the medina. Keiko enjoys drinking Japanese sake, hiking the trails of the Mojave Desert, and blogging about her adventures. She currently resides in Las Vegas with her husband, Scott, and an orange tabby named Buddy. **CrossingThePacific.com**

JEAN-BERNARD PONTHUS has devoted his life to Paris and some travels, though he has had a serious job in the French Post Office for 20 years. Exhibitions, learning new foreign languages, and sports are parts of his routine life— and literature is high on his scale of values. He was made a knight of the order of Arts and Letters by the French Government in July 2014.

MARY JEAN (MJ) PRAMIK contributed to the Travelers' Tales *"Venturing in"* series on the Canal du Midi, Greece, and Ireland and Wanderland Writers anthologies on Costa Rica, Bali, Andalusia, and Cuba. She has over thirty years' experience in professional science and medical writing at major biotechnology companies. MJ holds graduate degrees in biological sciences and writing, and has worked as a bench scientist at the University of California San Francisco. She moonlights as a medical writer in biotech, penning such scientific thrillers as *Norenthindrone, The First Three Decades*, the fast-paced history of the first birth control pill extracted from a Mexican yam. She's won several Solas Awards for her travel essays. Currently, she's wrapping up a novel, *GEM of Little Egypt Valley*, a family saga of immigration, coal mining, and reclaiming the earth. She blogs about travel and science at *Field Notes: Travel in Times of Catastrophic Change*, available at **MJPramik.com.**

ALLISON RENWICK was born in Detroit, so she has motor oil for blood and Motown for soul, but she's not a writer. She wanted to be an artist but didn't have the "inner necessity." Then, she wanted to be an architect but couldn't use a slide rule (it was the Dark Ages), so she became an art historian and loved every minute of it. Raised in Portland and spending her teaching career there, she retired to Ashland in 1997 where she gardens, studies Spanish, and—gasp!—may just try writing!

CHANT THOMAS: Born and raised in Washington, D.C., Chant Thomas has spent most of his life choosing adventure, homesteading in a wilderness canyon in the Siskiyou Mountains, working for conservation of wildlands, forests, mountains, and rivers. His writing ranges from scientific papers, conservation advocacy and short stories, to poetry and travel. Chant earned an M.S. in Environmental Education from the Biology Department of Southern Oregon University. He founded Dakubetede Environmental Education Programs, a university-accredited curriculum training Earth Activists, Earth Scientists and Earth Stewards. For twenty years, he operated Siskiyou Llama Expeditions, conducting recreational and educational wilderness treks in the State of Jefferson. Chant, with his wife Susanna, hosted an *Orion Society Forgotten Language* on their wilderness ranch in 1998. Chant is writing his first book as he and Susanna divide their time among Oregon, New Mexico, and Baja, living simply, immersed in Nature.

Writing beneath the palapa in Yelapa with Tim Cahill
Photo by Christina Ammon

MICHAEL SHAPIRO: Based in Sonoma County, California, Michael Shapiro writes about travel, environmental issues, and entertainment for national magazines and metro newspapers. Shapiro has written about cycling in Mongolia for the *Washington Post,* tasted tequila in Jalisco for *American Way,* and spoken with Jane Goodall for *The Explorers Journal.* His *National Geographic Traveler* feature, about Jan Morris' Wales, won the Bedford Pace grand award. His story about sustainable seafood in Vancouver earned the

2016 Explore Canada Award of Excellence. Shapiro's forthcoming book, *The Creative Spark,* a collection of interviews with musicians, authors, and other artists, comes out in Fall 2019. Among those profiled are Francis Ford Coppola, Amy Tan, Graham Nash, Merle Haggard and Barbara Kingsolver. Shapiro's first literary book, *A Sense of Place*, is a collection of interviews with the world's top travel authors including Bill Bryson, Frances Mayes, and Paul Theroux. Shapiro volunteers as a whitewater raft guide and sea kayak trip leader for a Northern California outfitter that takes special needs groups on outdoor adventures.

ANNE SIGMON flunked jump rope class in seventh grade and washed out of college PE. After college, she headed for San Francisco and a career in public relations. Exotic travel was the stuff of dreams until, at 38, she married Jack, took tea with erstwhile headhunters in Borneo and climbed Mt. Kilimanjaro at 43. Five years later, she was zapped by a career-ending stroke caused by an obscure autoimmune disease called Antiphospholipid Syndrome (APS). She may be stuck with blood thinners and a damaged brain, but she's still traveling to isolated regions ranging from Burma to Syria, Iran, and Uzbekistan. Her stories appear regularly in print and digital magazines and anthologies, most recently *Wanderlust*—adventure travel stories from GeoEx.com, *Wandering in Cuba: Revolution and Beyond,* and Bradt Guides' *To Oldly Go.* Anne has a BA in journalism and lives in Lafayette, CA, with her husband, Jack.

LAVINIA SPALDING is author of *Writing Away: A Creative Guide to Awakening the Journal-Writing Traveler,* and co-author of *With a Measure of Grace* and *This Immeasurable Place.* She is also series editor of *The Best Women's Travel Writing.* Lavinia wrote the introduction to the e-book edition of Edith Wharton's classic travelogue, *A*

Motor-Flight Through France, and her work appears in such publications as *AFAR, Yoga Journal, Sunset* magazine, *Airbnb Magazine, Tin House, Post Road,* the *San Francisco Chronicle, San Francisco* magazine, *The Guardian UK, World Hum,* and *Off Assignment.* She is a member of the San Francisco's Writers' Grotto and Peauxdunque Writers' Alliance, on faculty of the annual Book Passage Travel Writers & Photographers Conference, and co-founder of Weekday Wanderlust. She lives in New Orleans. Visit her at **www.LaviniaSpalding.com**.

PAUL WASZINK: A Dutch-born American now living in Cleveland, Ohio, with his beloved wife, artist Libby Chaney, Paul Waszink is now a re-emerging artist alongside being a semi-retired construction cost consultant. He has been a reading, writing, inventing, building, and making sort all his life. A lover of art, music, literature, architecture, history, occasional major travel, cats, and his family and friends, Paul firmly believes that close observation and listening, curiosity, reading the Mueller Report fully, and a good sense of humor are among the most crucial aspects of being human. With his crowded mind and an eye to making contributions—but increasingly intent on enjoying daily life and musing about the spiritual in most things—picture Paul Waszink paddling as lucidly as possible toward his dotage out on the Big River.

BRENDA WILSON presents us with a fun fusion of eclectic gifts from distant corners of the galaxy. She is a creative writer, by way of being a naturalist, herbalist, botanist, anatomist, astrologist, and massage therapist. She is a servant and observant of the wild creatures. She has worked with wild birds, wild plants, wild gardens, and wild humans of the best kind. She found herself whisked away to Yelapa, Mexico, by some of her favorite wild humans to serve and to write. She produced this story of beasts (during a wolf moon, in the year of the Dog) while doing massage service for the group of highly skilled travel writers. Brenda is honored to be included among the creative talent presented in this anthology. She earned an Associate's degree in English and Creative Writing and studied Shakespearean literature during a six-month, in-depth study in Cambridge, England.

GLORIA WILSON "You fit the profile," says a stranger ordering a drink next to me. At first, I was taken aback. What does that mean? But it is true: who and what I am is a teacher, spending my entire adult life teaching students with special needs and now teaching others to teach students with disabilities. My writing, mostly on the evolution of loss, is short, to the point, and for me, cathartic. I live in New York City, overlooking the East River and daily sunrises, and in the middle of museums, theatres, subways and crowds. I'm a professor at Hofstra University, mother to Caitlin and, of course, love adventures of many kinds.

JACQUELINE YAU writes travel, humor, and essays for publications including *Inspirato* and *Ensemble Vacations Magazine,* and for anthologies such as *Travelers' Tales China.* She is a regular contributor to the annual *Travel Guide to California* and a founding member of Townsend 11, a collective of eleven Northern California writers. They have published three anthologies. Jacqueline has spent many days pondering brand names, developing marketing strategies, and creating product launch plans for organizations large and small, from startups and non-profits to Fortune 500 companies. Some of her favorite experiences include learning the signature public radio voice as a news reporter for Hawaii Public Radio and deboning five hundred pounds of cooked chicken in a small family plant in Cleveland, Ohio, as a manufacturing intern for Nestlé USA. During the day, Jacqueline learns about the world of medicine, tracking discoveries as a writer for Stanford Medicine in donor relations. She recently returned from trekking in the Himalayan kingdom of Mustang in Nepal. She lives in Sonoma County, California, with her husband, where they enjoy hiking and cycling the wine country's backroads and going to local festivals. **JacquelineYau.com**

MICHELLE ZEIDMAN is an artist, writer, and avid traveler. Her adventures have taken her to 26 countries and counting. Michelle has snorkeled with humpback whales, flown her paraglider in the Himalayas, studied tropical ecology in the cloud forests of Costa Rica, and hiked hundreds of miles of trails across six continents. She has Masters degrees in Urban Planning (MUP) and Public Administration (MPA), and a Bachelor of Arts in Environmental Studies. Her art and jewelry can be viewed at **ModernNatureArt.com.**

Deep Travel in Nepal with Dot-Fisher Smith in 2014

Photo Credits

Want to Adventure With Us?

Visit **DeepTravelWorkshops.com**